indonesia

A Travel Portrait

indonesia
A Travel Portrait

Photography and Text by Kal Muller

PERIPLUS

EDITIONS

Distributors

Singapore & Malaysia: Berkeley Books Pte Ltd,
5 Little Road, #08-01, Singapore 536983

Indonesia: C.V. Java Books,
Jl. Gading Kirana Timur, Blok A13 No. 23, Jakarta 14240

Benelux: Nilsson & Lamm B.V., Pampuslaan
212-214, 1382 JS Weesp, The Netherlands

United Kingdom: Geo Center U.K. Ltd.,
The Viables Centre, Harrow Way, Basingstoke,
Hampshire RG22 4BJ

DEDICATION:
*To my children Nicole, Kalman and Andres,
with lots of love*

Front cover
*Sunset over Tanjung Pinang
harbor.*

Title spread
*Water buffalo head for home and
a bath after a day in the fields.
These good-natural animals,
called "the tractors of Indonesia,"
are indispensable in tilling the
terraced and irrigated fields prior
to planting rice. In some areas of
Indonesia water buffalo are
ritually sacrificed, with dozens of
the valuable animals being slaughtered to honor the death of a
prominent leader.*

Right
*Dressed in local finery, a smiling
performer dances in Bima, on
the island of Sumbawa. Though
the area is strongly Muslim,
ancient traditions such as Hindu-
influenced court dancers are kept
alive in Bima.*

Pages 6-7
*Central Java's Merapi volcano
gives off a plume of smoke as a
warning of its dormant destructive
power. While the volcanoes which
dominate the island are a potential threat to human life, the ash
from their eruptions has made
Javanese soil among the richest
on earth.*

Pages 8-9
*Dawn breaks over a quiet harbor
at Sape on the westernmost tip
of Sumbawa Island. Small-scale
fishing all over Indonesia provides
the essential protein to supplement
a rice-based diet.*

Pages 10-11
*The huge crater of Java's Bromo
volcano, lined with an ash plain
still filled with the night's mist,
spreads in front of an active cone
breathing out puffs of sulfur fumes.
The 300,000 Tenggerese inhabitants of the region hold an annual
rituel to appease the volcano.*

Pages 12-13
*The Moluccan Islands offer some
of the world's clearest waters for
swimming and diving. While these
islands still produce the cloves,
nutmeg and mace which drew
explorers and fortune seekers in
the past, the islands' economy is
one of subsistence farming and
fishing.*

Photography and text by Kal Muller

Layout by Pete Ivey

ISBN 962-593-018-3

SUMATRA World's fifth-largest island, the size of California. *Area*: 481,780 sq km. *Population*: 38 million. *Economy*: Based on oil, natural gas, rubber, palm oil and tobacco. *Ethnic groups*: Over 15, including the strongly Muslim Acehnese, the extroverted Bataks and the matriarchal Minangkabau.

BALI The best-known island in Indonesia, with over a million visitors annually. Called "Island of the Gods" for its many deities and Bali-Hindu religious festivals. *Area*: 5,532 sq km, the size of Hawaii. *Population*: 2.6 million. *Economy*: Wet-rice agriculture and tourism. *Ethnic group*: Balinese.

JAVA Includes the capital city of Jakarta—with 9 million inhabitants, the nation's political, administrative and economic center. *Area*: 130,398 sq km, the size of England. *Population*: 115 million. *Economy*: Wet-rice agriculture and manufacturing. *Ethnic groups*: Sundanese, Madurese and Javanese.

LESSER SUNDAS The chain arcing east from Bali to Timor, including five major and a dozen smaller islands. *Land area*: 82,741 sq km. *Population*: 7 million. *Economy*: Poor and arid region, primarily agricultural. *Ethnic groups*: Traditional animistic cultures, and several Christian ones.

Indonesia

KALIMANTAN The Indonesian portion of Borneo. *Area*: 549,032 sq km. *Population*: 9 million. *Economy*: Oil, natural gas and trading in the coastal cities; subsistence agriculture in the interior. *Ethnic groups*: Malays, Chinese and Bugis in the coastal cities; numerous Dayak groups in the interior.

MOLUCCAS A group of 1,000 islands, also known as the "Spice Isles." *Total land area*: 85,782 sq km. *Population*: 1.9 million. *Economy*: Subsistence agriculture and fishing. Once the world's sole supplier of cloves, nutmeg and mace. *Ethnic groups*: Over 50.

SULAWESI Formerly known as the Celebes. *Area*: 194,441 sq km, the size of Great Britain. *Population*: 13 million. *Economy*: Agricultural. *Ethnic groups*: Over 35. The Toraja in the south are known for their traditional houses and spectacular funerals. The coastal Bugis are the country's best sailors.

IRIAN JAYA The western half of New Guinea, world's second-largest island. *Area*: 419,660 sq km, the size of Spain, comprising 21% of Indonesia's land mass. *Population*: 1.6 million. *Economy*: Vast reserves of oil, copper and gold. Subsistence agriculture in highlands. *Ethnic groups*: Over 100.

INTRODUCTION

INDONESIA IS THE WORLD'S LARGEST ARCHIPELAGO, an enormous chain of islands spanning a distance of more than 5,000 kilometers (3,200 miles) along the equator, from Sumatra in the west to New Guinea in the east. To get a better idea of the country's immensity, consider that when superimposed on a map of Europe, Indonesia stretches from Ireland all the way to Iran. Over a map of North America, the archipelago reaches from California to Bermuda.

In each new survey, in fact, new islands seem to pop right out of the ocean (sometimes literally, as the result of volcanic eruptions). The latest count puts the total figure at well over 18,000 islands, ranging from huge New Guinea and Borneo—the second and third largest islands in the world after Greenland—to tiny atolls in the east, no more than mere specks in the ocean.

Indonesia's population keeps growing as well, despite the government's efforts at birth control. With 185 million citizens, Indonesia now ranks as the world's fifth most populous nation, just behind the United States. The majority, over 115 million, inhabit the island of Java, which is only about as large as England or New York State. At the other end of the spectrum, Irian Jaya (the Indonesian or western half of the huge island of New Guinea) has less than two million inhabitants while comprising over a fifth of the nation's total land area.

Inter-island migrations spanning several millennia and an uneven distribution of arable land and resources have combined with the archipelago's fragmented geography to produce a diversity of cultures and lifestyles found nowhere else in the world. Aeronautical engineers and computer programmers go to offices in cities like Jakarta, while primitive hunters, farmers and fishermen on New Guinea and other remote islands maintain millennia-old lifestyles. As city children watch American cop shows on TV and visit "Fantasy World" (Jakarta's version of Disneyland), others may be watching a neighborhood shaman in action or taking part in a ritual tribal battle fought with spears, bows and arrows.

An estimated 350 distinct ethnic groups inhabit Indonesia, each with its own language and cultural heritage. Several lifetimes of travel would be required to get even a general idea of this island nation's geographical and cultural richness.

A HISTORICAL GLIMPSE

The first known hominid inhabitant of Indonesia was the so-called "Java Man" or *Homo erectus* who lived here half a million years ago. Some 60,000 years ago, the ancestors of the present-day Papuans moved eastward through these islands, eventually reaching New Guinea and Australia some 30-40,000 years ago. Much later, in about the fourth millenium B.C., they were followed by the ancestors of the modern-day Malays, Javanese and other Malayo-Polynesian groups who now make up the bulk of Indonesia's population.

The Ice Ages aided these movements by lowering sea levels and reducing the distances separating many islands. But the outrigger canoe and simple sail were essential Malayo-Polynesian innovations that made such journeys possible. While at times sea levels dropped 100 meters (330 feet) below current levels, many long stretches of open sea still had to be crossed.

Man with his technology was in fact successful in migrating across the vast expanses of the region where most animals were not. This explains the many striking differences in the flora and fauna of the Asian mainland and Australia. Most notably, Asian mammals are placentals whereas those of Australia are marsupials. The Indonesian islands fall between these two distinct biogeographical regions, and indeed form a kind of transitional zone containing many unique and interesting species found nowhere else—giant lizards, rare flowers, strange insects, beautiful birds, exotic spice and fruit trees, and more.

Top
A Batak lady from Sumatra smiles through betel-nut-stained teeth and gums. Converted by Protestant missionaries in the latter part of the 19th century, the extroverted Bataks now channel their overflowing energy into rousing songs, as well as military and business pursuits.

Above
The 30-odd million Sundanese of West Java speak their own language and hold to a culture distinct from the Javanese. They have a love for bright colors and are fond of their traditional music and local dances.

Trade contacts with India, China and the mainland of Southeast Asia brought outside cultural and religious influences to Indonesia. Early leaders were able to reinforce their control of rice production and trade by promoting new Indian concepts of divine kingship. One of the first of the great Indianized empires, known to us now as Sriwijaya, was located on the coast of Sumatra around the strategic Straits of Malacca—serving as the hub of a trading network that reached to many parts of the archipelago more than a thousand years ago.

Meanwhile, on neighboring Java, large kingdoms in the interior of the island erected scores of exquisite religious monuments, such as the marvelous Borobudur, the largest Buddhist monument in the world. The last and most powerful of these early Hindu-Javanese kingdoms, 14th-century Majapahit, once controlled or influenced much of what is now Indonesia, maintaining contacts with trading outposts as far away as the west coast of New Guinea.

Muslim Indian traders, following routes established long before the time of Mohammed, began spreading Islam through Indonesia in the eighth and ninth centuries. By the time Marco Polo visited north Sumatra at the end of the 13th century, the first Islamic states were already established there. Soon afterwards, rulers on Java's north coast adopted the new creed and conquered the Hindu-based Majapahit Empire in the Javanese hinterland. The faith gradually spread throughout the archipelago, and Indonesia is today the world's largest Islamic nation.

Indonesia's abundant spices first brought Portuguese merchants to the key trading port of Malacca in 1511. Prized for their flavor, spices such as cloves, nutmeg and mace were also believed to cure everything from the plague to venereal disease, and were literally worth their weight in gold. The Dutch eventually wrested control of the spice trade from the Portuguese, and the tenacious Dutch East India Company (known by the initials VOC) established a spice monopoly which lasted well into the 18th century. During the 19th century, the Dutch began sugar and coffee cultivation on Java, which was soon providing three-fourths of the world's supply of coffee—hence the expression "a cup of Java."

By the turn of the 20th century, nationalist stirrings, brought about by nearly three centuries of oppressive colonial rule, began to challenge the Dutch presence in Indonesia. A four-year guerilla war led by nationalists against the Dutch on Java after World War II, along with successful diplomatic maneuverings abroad, helped bring about independence. The Republic of Indonesia, officially proclaimed on August 17th, 1945, gained sovereignty four years later.

During the first two decades of independence, the republic was dominated by the charismatic figure of Sukarno, one of the early nationalists who had been imprisoned by the Dutch. The current leader, General Suharto, eased Sukarno from power in 1967. The policies of fiscal responsibility and development initiated by Suharto's New Order government continue today.

Indonesia's economy was sustained throughout the 1970s almost exclusively by oil exports. Today, processed timber, fish, shrimp, minerals, fertilizer and textiles have greatly diversified the export trade, and a crash program of intensive rice production has made Indonesia self-sufficient in her staple crop. Production of steel, chemicals, cement, processed foods and other items has dramatically decreased a dependence on imports, and tourism now gives the economy a much-needed boost.

Problems remain, however. Communications across the vast archipelago present major difficulties, slowly being resolved through a satellite telecommunications network, more frequent scheduled flights, and improved shipping and roads. Although birth control has begun to win acceptance, there are too many people and too few jobs. Most of the unemployed are on Java, and massive transmigration schemes have relieved only a fraction of the island's population problems.

Indonesia is nevertheless a young, rapidly developing nation full of hope for the future. GNP growth rates are currently in the healthy range of 5 to 7 percent per annum; new houses and factories proliferate. A visit to Indonesia will convince the traveller that the country is well on its way to achieving the goal implied in its national motto—*Binneka Tunggal Ika*—meaning "Unity in Diversity."

INDONESIA AT A GLANCE

Indonesia is divided into 27 provinces for administrative purposes, but the archipelago falls naturally into eight major islands and island groups. The large islands are Sumatra, Java, Kalimantan (Borneo), Sulawesi (The Celebes) and Irian Jaya (New Guinea). The smaller ones can then be divided into two main groups: the Moluccas to the northeast, and the Lesser Sunda chain east of Bali. The tiny island of Bali is unique in several ways and can be classed separately.

Sumatra. The huge, 1,700-kilometer-long island of Sumatra lies along a northwest-to-southeast axis that is bisected by the equator, and forms a kind of western backbone for the Indonesian archipelago. A great volcanic chain, the Bukit Barisan, runs the entire length of the island.

On the west coast, the mountains fall abruptly to the sea, while to the east they ease gradually down to plains and a broad fringe of coastal mangroves. During the Ice Ages, Sumatra was connected to Java, Borneo and the mainland, forming an enormous sub-continent the size of India. Rising seas have left it bordering two narrow straits (Sunda and Malacca) that for centuries have served as vital sea links between the Far East and the West.

Sriwijaya, the first great Indonesian empire, had its capital near present-day Palembang in southern Sumatra, and controlled the straits with a powerful navy. The northern part of the island, through which the Islamic faith first spread into Indonesia, is an area which remains devoutly Muslim today.

Visitors flock to the area around scenic Lake Toba, a jewel-like crater lake set in the northern highlands which covers an area four times the size of Singapore. According to geologists, Toba was created in pre-historic times by the greatest volcanic explosion the world has ever seen.

The Batak people who live around Lake Toba continued to practice cannibalism until well into the 19th century, when Western missionaries persuaded them to alter their diet. The Minangkabau, inhabitants of the spectacular highlands to the south and west, are noted for their spicy cuisine, their distinctive houses with multi-peaked roofs, and a unique social system based on matrilineal descent.

Java. The political and commercial hub of Indonesia, Java crowds over 115 million people, or 65 percent of the nation's population, onto just 7 percent of its land area. Though densely inhabited, the island contains numerous beautifully terraced ricefields yielding prodigious quantities of grain. Its magnificent volcanic highlands are still rather sparsely populated. The capital city of Jakarta, located on Java's northwest coast, is home to over 9 million people. The country's intellectual, political and economic elite merge here with immigrants from all parts of the country, who flock to Jakarta in search of job opportunities and big-city excitement.

The rest of the island is divided into three provinces. The Sundanese are the dominant presence in West Java, and maintain their own distinctive language and culture. The provinces of Central and East Java are inhabited by the ethnic Javanese, who make up the majority of Indonesia's total population, as well as the nation's political and military elite.

The world-renowned Buddhist monument of Borobudur remains the top attraction for visitors to Java. The Hindu shrine at Prambanan and a host of other monuments scattered across the island give further evidence of the island's fascinating history. The bustling city of Yogyakarta, nestling in the shadow of towering Merapi volcano in Central Java, houses the court of Sultan Hamengkubuwono, where ancient traditions are strictly observed in a highly formal setting.

To the east, the spectacular beauty of of the huge crater and active volcano of

Top
A Balinese pemangku, *or lower-level priest, takes a break from his ritual duties to lovingly hold his granddaughter. The government's birth-control program, recognized by the U.N. for its effectiveness, is helping to reduce over-population in crowded areas such as Bali and Java.*

Above
A Buginese girl, dressed in aristocratic finery. Sharing Sulawesi's southern peninsula with the Toraja, the Buginese sailed to all corners of the archipelago for trade, and founded royal dynasties in Kalimantan, Malaysia and the Riau Islands.

Top

A man from Timor Island. Located in eastern Indonesia only 500 kilometers northwest of Darwin, Australia, Timor is arid and agriculturally poor. Early Chinese and Javanese traders were lured to Timor by the island's abundant supply of fragrant sandalwood.

Above

Earlobes stretched by heavy metal rings, once the fashion among the Dayaks of Kalimantan, are fast going out of style. Many Dayak ladies now have their lobes cut in deference to modern taste.

Bromo forms the focus of religious activities for the Tenggerese people who live here. Each year, a multitude of offerings are hurled into the smouldering volcano.

Bali. This tiny island of 2.6 million inhabitants, Indonesia's best-known spot to outsiders, attracts hundreds of thousands of visitors a year. Balinese culture is truly unique in the archipelago. The island's traditional religion is a combination of spirit and ancestor cults within a Hindu-Javanese framework, rich in spectacular rituals of exorcism and renewal. It is believed that when Islam conquered Java in the 15th and 16th centuries, the Hindu-Javanese elite fled to Bali to preserve its refined and sophisticated culture.

Westerners have been enchanted with Bali since a handful of sailors from the first Dutch expedition in 1597 chose to stay behind rather than return to Holland. Bali's bare-breasted women were a prime attraction for Victorian Europeans. Later, foreign visitors began to appreciate its scenic beauty and its traditions.

Bali was conquered by the Dutch in the early 20th century, but aside from administrative control they instituted few changes. Widows were forbidden to throw themselves on their husbands' funerary pyres, and young ladies had to cover up their bosoms so the Dutch soldiers could keep their minds on military matters. It is ironic that the Balinese now regularly come to check out bare-breasted Westerners on the free-wheeling beach at Kuta.

In spite of all the attention that Bali receives from hordes of tourists, it retains much of its charm and magic, and its culture remains surprisingly alive. The Balinese have a proud sense of their own identity and a tolerant view of others.

Kalimantan (Indonesian Borneo). While much of Kalimantan, which covers three-fourths of the huge island of Borneo, is poorly suited for agriculture, it contains great reserves of natural resources including oil, natural gas, coal, gold and uranium. Rich timberland also provides much-needed jobs and revenue to the region, though the destruction of the island's invaluable rainforest is bringing severe ecological problems in its wake.

The larger cities all lie on or near the coast. Few highways exist, and water-borne transportation moves cargo and passengers up and down the major rivers—the Mahakam, Barito, Kahayan and Kapuas.

The Dayak peoples of the interior preserve many of their ancient ways in spite of their Western clothing, outboard-powered canoes and nominal Christianity. In some areas, dancers wearing huge masks celebrate the agricultural cycle, attracting good spirits and chasing away evil ones. Funerals of important men are celebrated with animal sacrifices under the direction of shamans.

Sulawesi (The Celebes). Sulawesi sprawls to the east of Kalimantan like an orchid or a headless octopus—four long peninsulas extending from a central core of mountains. Each arm of the island is so distinctive that in fact the Portuguese for a long time thought it was a cluster of separate islands.

There are scores of distinct ethnic groups in Sulawesi. The Toraja in the interior of South Sulawesi maintain many of their old traditions while professing the Protestant faith. Spectacular funerary rituals here culminate in the slaughter of dozens—sometimes even hundreds—of prized water buffalo. Life-sized wooden figures representing the spirits of the deceased perch on cliff-side gravesites. These figures receive offerings from their descendants in return for providing good health and abundant harvests of rice.

Traditional Toraja houses are massive works of art, with peaked roofs and panels of colorful carvings, complemented with wooden water buffalo heads and vertical rows of horns. The Toraja reap two or even three harvests a year from their fertile soils, which are beautifully terraced and irrigated.

To the south and east, the Bugis people continue to build the sailing craft (now equipped with large diesel engines) which transport much of Indonesia's inter-island cargo. Ancient mariners, the Bugis were already sailing to Australia centuries ago to collect sea cucumbers much in demand by Chinese gastronomes. The Bugis developed their own phonetic alphabet and have spread throughout Indonesia, establishing their sea-based settlements along the coasts.

North Sulawesi is the home of the Minahassa people, centered around the town of Manado. The white-skinned Minahassan girls are said to be the most beautiful in the country. Experienced divers consider the underwater scenery off the islands near Manado among the best in the world.

The Lesser Sundas. The Lesser Sunda Islands form a long chain to the east of Bali, comprising scores of islands large and small. While its poor soils and dry climate are not well suited for agriculture, traditional ritual events held here are among the most spectacular in Indonesia.

On Sumba Island, horsemen armed with spears fight ritual battles. Megalithic stone tombs, many with artistically carved headpieces weighing several tons, shelter the remains of powerful deceased nobles. Funerary rites culminate in the slaughter of water buffalo, horses, pigs and dogs, all consumed in feasts to honor the deceased. Sumba's colorful cloths, sought by collectors around the world, are still woven and dyed by the ancient *ikat* technique.

Traditional weavings are also found on the neighboring island of Flores. This long, mountainous island holds a unique attraction: the colored volcanic lakes known as Keli Mutu. Linked closely together, the three lakes are all of different hues, ranging from darkish red to a light turquoise. On the western end of Flores, men hold traditional fights with long whips. A deeply scarred back shows bravery and appeals to the fairer sex.

To the west of Flores, the island of Komodo is the habitat of the world's largest lizard—the 3-meter (ten feet) long, 150-kilo (330 lbs) Komodo dragon—a real prehistoric monster with a long, yellow, forked tongue and armor-plated body.

To the east of Flores, the island of Lembata is home to a tough breed of fishermen. Going after any large fish or whale, the men actually jump into the water with their harpoons to give them maximum force and accuracy. The large island of Timor at the eastern end of the archipelago, also known for its weavings, hosts many traditional events, including vigorous war dances.

The Moluccas. This chain of over 1,000 islands offers brilliant white sand beaches and crystalline waters teeming with an incredible variety of fish and coral. The snorkeling and scuba diving here are world-class, and so is the scenery. Vegetation-clad volcanoes rise dramatically from the sea at Banda, Ternate, Tidore and Makian. Many of the volcanoes are still active today, occasionally erupting to awaken normally drowsy coastal settlements.

Irian Jaya (Indonesian New Guinea). Unbelievable sights await the visitor in the highlands of Irian Jaya. The fertile Baliem Valley, "discovered" only in 1938, was then home to 60,000 stone-age farmer-warriors. Dani tribesmen here sport bright yellow penis gourds while the ladies make do with plain grass skirts. Today, the Dani still grow their staple sweet potatoes in irrigated networks of raised mounds, while cash income derives from vegetables sold at the market in Wamena. There are no roads into the highlands, but a regular scheduled flight connects Wamena with the provincial capital of Jayapura.

Ritual warfare, over matters such as stolen pigs, wives, or disputed land, still occasionally takes place, with modern steel axes complementing the old spear, bow and arrow. Visitors have nothing to fear, however. On the contrary, beautifully caparisoned Dani warriors ready for combat are only too happy to pose for photos. In battle, one's appearance is just as important as one's fighting ability.

Most of Irian's rich mineral resources await development, with the notable exception of Freeport's incredible copper mine at Tembagapura, located at an elevation of some 3,800 meters, in the midst of some of the world's most remote and inhospitable terrain. The mine lies near Jaya Summit, which at 5,000 meters (16,000 feet) is Southeast Asia's highest peak, rising straight up from the coastal lowlands and swamps, and capped by permanent snowfields.

Top
Proudly wearing a gold helmet given to his ancestors by the Portuguese during the 16th century, Dom Bartolomeu retains a large measure of respect among the inhabitants of the region of Maumere on Flores Island. Portuguese traders and missionaries were the first Europeans in eastern Indonesia.

Above
A breastplate of tiny cowrie shells—formerly used as money and as a mark of prestige—adorns a Dani tribesman from Irian Jaya's Baliem Valley. Many Dani men still prefer penis sheaths to shorts.

Preceding pages
Ricefields shimmering in the early morning sunlight in the Minangkabau highlands near Bukittingi in Sumatra. The fields are contoured to prevent erosion and to fit slope patterns.

Top
The fiercely independent Acehnese, living in northernmost Sumatra, were defeated but never fully conquered by the Dutch. The central government in Jakarta has granted them special autonomous status. The traditional dress is now worn only for special occasions. Indonesia is the world's largest Muslim nation, with over 85 percent of its 185 million people embracing the faith of Mohammed. Brought by traders from India and Arabia, Islam entered Indonesia through Aceh, and the Acehnese are still among the country's strictest practitioners of the faith.

Left and above
Banda Aceh's principal mosque, Mesjit Baturrachman, graces the center of town as an oasis of tranquility. It was built by the Dutch in 1879 as a peace offering, on the site of the grand mosque which they had destroyed. Combining stylistic elements from Arabia and India, this mosque is among Indonesia's most exquisite religious buildings.

Below right
Lake Toba, spreading over 1,000 square kilometers, is the largest body of fresh water in Southeast Asia, covering four times the area of Singapore. The north Sumatran lake, located at an altitude of 900 meters, is actually a 450-meter deep crater formed by a huge volcanic eruption. Lake water, cascading to the coast along the Asahan River, is dammed for hydroelectric power. The one million Toba Batak living around the lake are dynamic and extroverted. In the late 19th century, Protestant missionaries succeeded in converting most of the Bataks and stopping wide-spread ritual cannibalism. Many other aspects of Batak culture, however, have been preserved, including traditional architecture (below left) and local styles of ceremonial dress.

Above
The tranquil waters of Lake Meninjau fill a vast volcanic crater. Located some 40 kilometers west of Bukittinggi, the crater is reached by a road which rises 600 meters through 44 hairpin switch-backs. An inspiration to poets and philosophers on account of its beauty, the lake also offers mundane diversions such as swimming, boating, skiing and fishing.

Top right
*Minangkabau women in west Sumatra
retain a predominant role in their
matriarchal culture. Husbands live in the
wife's house and work for the mother-in-law.
Many problems have resulted from trying to
reconcile Islamic patriarchy with local
customs, particularly in the matter of
inheritance.*

Above
*The best example of traditional
Minangkabau architecture is a replica of King
Adityawarman's Palace, which burned to the
ground in 1976. Located at Pagaruyung near
the town of Batusongkar in the heart of the
Minangkabau highlands, this baroque
wooden structure, known as Istana
Pagaruyung, marks the site of a
former raja's court.*

Preceding pages
Jakarta's Istiqlal Mosque is the largest mosque in southeast Asia, and one of the world's biggest places of worship.

Left
Colorful August 17th Independence Day parade winds its way through downtown Jakarta, past a Soviet-style statue from the Sukarno era. The bronze figures were fashioned by sculptor Edi Sunarso for the 1962 Asian games.

Above
Twilight traffic in Jakarta near the Monas, or National Monument. In the background is the Istiqlal Mosque.

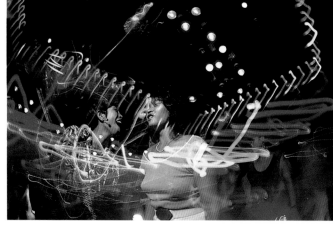

Top
President Suharto, Indonesia's ruler since 1967, smiles with his wife from a downtown Jakarta billboard promoting agricultural development.

Above
A family out for a spin on dad's motorbike. Increasing affluence among Jakarta's middle class has led to greater numbers of private vehicles, as well as frequent traffic jams. Jakarta's population of 9 million increases daily with hordes of job-seekers, mostly from overpopulated rural Java.

Top
A member of Indonesia's elite Rangers Unit stands guard at the National Palace.

Above
At the Tanamur disco, expats and locals gather amidst flashing lights and loud music. Many foreigners live in Jakarta, where international companies situate their Indonesian headquarters.

Left

Anak Krakatoa volcano, just off west Java. Formed in 1927, this "baby" is named after the volcano which exploded in 1883 with a force of 100,000 A-bombs, killing 36,000 people and causing tidal waves up to 40 meters high. Anak (Son of) Krakatoa rises up 200 meters from the narrow sea passage between Java and Sumatra.

Above

Tea plantations carpet vast areas of West Java, providing jobs and hard cash from exports. Large-scale tea planting was introduced by the Dutch on Java during the 19th century under a forced cultivation program.

Right

Ram fights, unique to west Java, are a popular form of entertainment. The rams charge each other across the arena to butt heads with a sickening crack. Opponents repeat their charges until one retreats to the jeers of the crowd, leaving the field to the winner.

Below right

The Badui, an isolated mountain tribe, shun most contacts with the outside world. Living a life of mystic contemplation, they strive to bring harmony to the island and the country. The three inner Badui villages, where all wear white clothing, are off-limits to outsiders, who may only briefly visit the black-clad outer Badui.

Preceding pages and above
The Buddhist temple of Borobudur emerges from the dawn mist. The largest Buddhist temple in the world, Borobudur is also the biggest monument in the southern hemisphere. Located in south-central Java near the town of Yogyakarta, Borobudur was built by the Sailendra dynasty between A.D. 778 and 850 as an illuminated holy book on the Mahayana Buddhist faith. Its scope and detail stagger the imagination: over a million blocks of stone with some 1,500 large relief panels blend into a harmonious represen- tation of the Buddhist cosmos. Due to a change in religion and dynasty, Borobudur was abandoned shortly after it was completed; volcanic eruptions and tropical vegetation then turned the temple into an overgrown hill. Dormant for over a millennium, Borobudur was rediscovered during the British occupation of Java in the Napoleonic era, and restored to its former splendor by a 10-year, multi-million dollar project completed in 1983.

Left
This 2.5- meter statue of Buddha at Mendut temple dates from the 9th century. Mendut is the center of Waicak Day, the Buddhist festival held during the full-moon period in May.

Right
Prambanan, a Hindu temple built between the 8th and 10th centuries, is the mausoleum of King Balitung of the Mataram dynasty, who believed himself to be a reincarnation of Shiva. The central portion of the temple, dedicated to Shiva, is 50 meters high. Chambers within the temple hold large stone sculptures of Shiva and other Hindu deities while relief panels (above) on the outside depict scenes from the Ramayana epic. Here, Rama kills the golden deer whose shape was taken by an evil character.

Above
The kraton, *or sultan's royal palace, of Yogyakarta is a sacred walled world of its own where pre-Muslim and even pre-Hindu rituals and values preserve the flower of traditional Javanese culture. While other sultanates have been abolished in Indonesia, the* kraton *in Yogya keeps its special status thanks to its historical importance as well as to the unstinting support its sultan gave to the anti-Dutch revolution which led to the country's independence.*

Left
Inside the kraton, *a special open-air pavilion serves as a reception area for honored guests. The court attendant is clad in a batik sarong and headpiece appropriate to his rank.*

Below left
At a classical Javanese wedding, the bride feeds the groom to show her devotion to him. Her coiffure imitates an ancient Chinese fashion.

Above
Dancers in Central Java must undergo years of training with specialized teachers in order to perform for highly demanding local audiences. The sophisticated dances were reserved exclusively for court ladies until the early part of this century.

Left
The central figure of the kraton's reception pavilion features Kala Makala, the Lord of the Jungle, along with a Javanese symbol representing time.

Below left
A small procession with sacred water and daily offerings crosses one of the kraton's courtyards. Propitiating ancient spirits, an essential task in the kraton, does not conflict with the Muslim faith of the local population, whose devotion to Islam is far from fanatical.

Above and left
Stately classical dances are an integral component of traditional Javanese culture. This dance form emphasizes slow, controlled motion, pauses, silences and subtle expressions. Classical dancing is now quite popular in Java, with professional troupes putting on public and private performances. The courts of Yogyakarta and Solo are considered the standard-bearers of this art form.

Above

A kraton *attendant holds two elaborate* wayang kulit *figures made from water buffalo skin. The* wayang kulit *shadow puppet theater remains the most popular form of mass entertainment in Java. The backlit figures, manipulated by a* dalang *or master puppeteer, cast shadows on a transparent screen facing the audience (right). While incorporating the Hindu legends of the Ramayana and the Mahabarata, the characters and actions of the* wayang kulit, *which have been performed for at least a thousand years, remain essentially Javanese. Both didactic and entertaining, the shows were used in the past by Muslims to teach the faith. Today some performances are scripted to boost government policies such as birth control.*

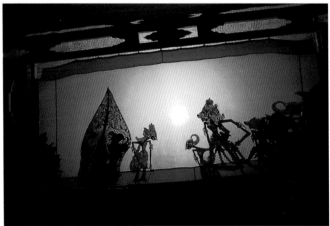

Left
Peering out of a colorful oxcart, the driver's assistant relaxes on the way to a hauling job. Carts drawn by bulls or water buffalo are a common sight in rural Java.

Below
Heading to morning market with a load of homemade pottery on dirt roads between flooded rice paddies requires balance and experience. When a car or truck must squeeze by, priority is usually given to pedestrians.

Bottom
Horsecarts are popular in many Javanese cities and rural areas, as they can carry more than becaks *(pedicabs), and are effective on poor roads.*

Above
Railroad buffs can ride on a 15-kilometer-long cog railway running from Ambarawa, located south of Semarang on Java's north coast, to the mountain villages of Jambu and Bedono. This wood-burning steam locomotive, which dates from 1903, is lovingly maintained. In Solo, a colorful becak *passes in front of a mosque graced with Moorish arches and flowing Arabic script (right).* Becaks *offer cheap transportation in much of Java. Although some Indonesians consider the vehicles demeaning to the driver,* becaks *give gainful employment to thousands while providing inexpensive, non-polluting transportation. They are especially useful in remote places where few are willing to risk motor vehicles.*

Above

Set against the background of majestic volcanoes, a tobacco field produces fine leaves for locally made kretek *cigarettes. The enormously popular sweet-smelling clove-and-tobacco* kretek *is the aroma of Indonesia; its onomatopoeic name comes from the crackling sound of the burning cloves. Kretek factories are concentrated in the Kudus area of Central Java. Special tax concessions, meant to absorb excess labor, encourage the hand-rolling of* kreteks *(left). Single factories turn out well over a million of the handmade cigarettes each day, rolled by female workers who average about 5,000 apiece. Machines may be switched on only after the hand-rolled quota has been met. The world's sole source of cloves until the 18th century, Indonesia is still the leading producer of the spice. Indonesians' devotion to* kretek *cigarettes has also made the country the world's largest importer of cloves, mostly from Zanzibar.*

Above
Rich as Java's soil may be, there is not enough of it to feed the island's 115 million inhabitants. Every bit of usable earth is carefully terraced and irrigated for maximum efficiency. While rice dominates, corn and other vegetables help diversify land use.

Right
Clad in the traditional batik sarong, three happy Javanese women make their way home from morning market. A strip of batik *cloth is used to tie loads around the back, leaving the hands free. Small markets scattered around the countryside allow farmers to sell their produce close to home, saving the expense of the trip to a city.*

45

Preceding pages
Outriggered fishing boats set out from Bali's south coast at dusk, taking advantage of a moonless night to fish with pressure lamps. Most Balinese fishing boats have magical eyes painted on the prow to spot and avert potential disasters.

Right
A beautiful young Balinese girl smiles shyly during the celebration rituals of her her first menstruation, an essential rite of passage.

Below
Small shrines are part of the temple complex of Pura Luhur on Mt. Batukau, a place of worship whose importance dates back centuries before the arrival of Hinduism in Bali. Special natural spots such as springs, crags and mountains are honored for the spirits who inhabit them.

Above
Besakih, Bali's "Mother Temple," sits 900 meters up on the slopes of sacred Gunung Agung, at 3,142 meters the highest mountain on the island. Besakih is the grandest and most important of Bali's countless temples.

Right
A procession winds its way from Besakih to the sea during the Eka Dasa Rudra ceremony. Performed only once every century, or during great crises, the ritual is designed to purify the whole universe and to restore the cosmic equilibrium between good and evil.

Below right
The typical procession for a temple ritual features girls and women, dressed in their best, balancing elaborate offerings for deities and ancestral spirits. After the spirits have absorbed the essence of the offerings, humans may feast on the substance.

Above
An elaborate lion-dragon sarcophagus, containing the remains of the Dutch artist Rudolph Bonnet, burns during the funerary rituals for the Raja of Ubud. Bonnet lived in Ubud for many years and was very good friends with the Raja; he requested that his remains be burned at the same time as his friend's.

Left
The Balinese believe that cremation of the body is essential to release the soul before reincarnation can take place.

Below left
A colorful papier mâché monster stares from the Raja's funerary tower to frighten away evil spirits which could disrupt proceedings.

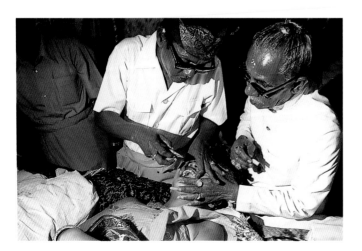

Left

A ritual fight with thorny leaves in the Bali Aga village of Tenganan. Human blood falling on the ground is the best possible offering to the spirits. The Bali Aga, among the most traditional of the Balinese, follow many pre-Hindu beliefs.

Below left

An adolescent undergoes a coming-of-age ritual where the upper incisors are filed down slightly. It is believed that this will eradicate uncontrolled, animal-like behavior and turn the youngster into a well-adjusted adult.

Above

Thundering water-buffalo races near Negara, on Bali's south-west coast, put emphasis not only on speed but also on appearance and gracefulness. The race, held after the rice harvest, covers a meandering two kilometers among rice paddies and back roads.

Above
Located between the islands of Flores and Sumbawa, Komodo Island is a favorite spot for experienced divers.

Left
Mineral deposits give the volcanic crater lakes of Keli Mutu (Central Flores) their gem-like appearance.

Left
Komodo dragons enjoying a goat meal. Prehistoric lizards weighing up to 150 kilograms (330 lbs) and reaching three meters in length, Komodo dragons prey on deer, wild cattle, boar and the occasional human. Unarticulated jaws allow for huge bites, and powerful gastric juices dissolve everything but hair.

Left
Savu islanders collect the juice of the lontar *palm twice a day. The juice is the island's dietary staple, and is also fermented to make palm wine.*

Above
The harpooner of a small whaling boat jumps for added strength and accuracy. Equipped with woven leaf sails, these boats ply Lembata Island's southern shores in search of whales, sharks, manta rays, sailfish and other large quarry.

Right
A sperm whale is towed ashore for butchering.

Below right
A Lombok Island fisherman casts his net into the sunset. Fishing is a primary source of sustenance on land-poor Lombok.

Above

Sumba's animist merapu *priests ride their horses to a sacred spot to communicate with spirits. Most inhabitants of West Sumba follow ancestral ways in spite of decades-long efforts by missionaries to convert them.*

Right

Sumba's annual pasola *ritual pits men from coastal villages against inlanders. Fighting with spears on horseback, opponents are sometimes wounded and even killed despite a government ban on sharp points. The goal of the "battle" is to spill blood on the ground, as an offering to the spirits for abundant harvests and good health.*

Above
A merapu *priest scans the water for* nyale *sea worms, whose yearly journey to shore is part of the lunar cycle which inaugurates the* pasola *ritual. Priests make divinations based on the shape, size and color of the* nyale.

Right
Singing of his clan's ancestors, a merapu *celebrates the lunar new year. University graduates and government officials are among the followers of this traditional religion.*

Above
Two men of Western Flores square off in a ritual whip fight which often results in deep open wounds. The fights are a feature of traditional weddings in the Manggarai region of Flores, where bride's and groom's clans are pitted against each other.

Right
A dancer from eastern Flores performs a warrior number, clenching an arrow in his teeth while wielding a bow and an old sword.

Below right
Girls in hand-woven sarongs provide accompaniment for a dance in Timor.

Above
Two Sumbawa Islanders engage in a ritual boxing match where making the opponent bleed is the name of the game. Blood on the rice stalks clenched in their hands is a thanksgiving offering to the spirits for an abundant harvest.

Right
Two warriors from Timor strike a heroic pose with their ancient swords during a ritual war dance.

Above
The floating market at Banjarmasin, the bustling capital of the province of South Kalimantan, is a jam of boats as shoppers and merchants buy and sell an astonishing variety of produce from upriver. The Banjarese have created arable land from much of the brackish tidal swamp that surrounds the city, and now the area produces bumper crops of rice and corn as well as vegetables, tangerines, oranges, coconuts and even cattle.

Left
The Barito River is market, highway, and bathtub for the people of Banjarmasin. Squatting by the river in front of the stilted houses that line the Barito, the Banjarese perform their morning ablutions before the start of another day.

Above

The Mahakam River is East Kalimantan's greatest waterway. It springs to life deep in the heart of Borneo, and winds 650 kilometers (400 mi) before reaching the Makassar Strait. Peaceful and crystal clear in the highlands, the river roars through a vicious stretch of rapids before slowing and widening into muddy brown loops as it nears the coast.

Left

A guide paddles his small craft near the headwaters of the Kayan River, deep in Borneo's interior. The Apokayan—"high plateau Kayan"—is one of East Kalimantan's most remote regions. A stretch of fierce rapids cuts the area off from the coast, and the Dayaks who live here still follow many of their old ways.

Left
The hudoq *dance, with huge and horrific carved masks, is performed at key points in the rice-growing to keep maleficent spirits from taking over the "soul" of the rice.*

Above
This hudoq *dancer is a Bahau Dayak from Long Hubung on the great Mahakam River in East Kalimantan. Although the Bahau retain many aspects of their traditional culture, they are today almost all Christians. The dancer pictured here is in fact a Catholic priest—a testament to the tradition of tolerance among Roman Catholic missionaries.*

Right
A Kenyah Dayak chief in full regalia. If the status of this aristocrat were not obvious from his bearing, then it could be determined by the special tattoos, beaded headdress and cape cut from the skin of a clouded leopard.

Below
Although today this Kenyah war dance is strictly for entertainment, in the past the actions mimed here would have counterparts on the field of battle. The Dayak mandau, *or short sword, poised to strike the dancer's opponent, was a head-hunting weapon nonpareil. When Europeans came to Borneo, they found the Dayaks to be extremely skilled at forging iron—a* mandau *blade could cut a Dutch musket in two.*

Above
The climax of the Erau Festival, at Tenggarong in East Kalimantan, comes when a pair of celebrants cuts off the head of a symbolic dragon, allowing its body to float down the great Mahakam River to the sea. The periodic festival celebrates the founding of Tenggarong on September 28, 1782, when the Sultan of Kutai moved the seat of his kingdom here. The festival is a five-day affair, with canoe races, sports, frenzied Dayak dances, and the slaughter of a water buffalo.

Left
The Javanese influence in Tenggarong culture shows through in the dances performed at the festival.

Top and above
Dayak art is famous among collectors world-wide. This fantastic sculpture and painting decorate a Kenyah longhouse in the interior of East Kalimantan. The Kenyah are renowned for their bright and colorful motifs. Even the roofs of the longhouse—a stilted dwelling sometimes hundreds of meters long and housing an entire village—are occasionally graced with carvings.

Above right
A Dayak woman literally carries the family wealth on her back, in the form of elaborate, beaded baby carriers. The honey bear and leopard teeth, old colonial coins, and beads that adorn this particularly fine example are designed to keep evil spirits from the vulnerable child. Fine trade beads (in double rows above and below the coins) were highly prized by the Dayaks, and there are accounts of single beads worth an entire village.

Above
Sunset on the harbor entrance at Ujung Pandang, Sulawesi's main city. Known as Makassar for most of its history, as the seat of the powerful Gowa sultanate, Ujung Pandang is today the commercial hub of eastern Indonesia.

Left
Bugis schooners dock at Ujung Pandang. Driven by sail for centuries, most vessels today are equipped with diesel engines.

Top
Dawn over the Toraja ricefields. Surplus grain is exported to Java. Descendants of nobles and slaves (above) are equal today in the eyes of Sulawesi law.

Above
A wooden sled smooths a Toraja rice paddy before the planting of rice shoots.

Left
From their cliffside graves, ancestral spirits of the Toraja clan watch over the harvests of their descendants.

Top
Life-size wooden statues of the deceased crowd before the graves. These sacred Toraja sculptures, called tau tau, *are much in demand by art collectors.*

Above
A carved wooden coffin holds the bones of several Toraja generations, their skulls neatly arranged by a thoughtful clan member.

Top
The facades of Toraja houses are covered with carved and painted panels featuring water buffalo heads, the symbol of wealth.

Right
A typical Toraja village has two facing rows of houses.

Above
Family rice barns, a smaller version of the houses, sometimes sport painted panels with a sense of humor.

Top
A pig slung on a bamboo pole is brought to a temporary funeral ground for sacrifice. After the sacrifice, guests staying in huts built specially for the funeral ceremony will eat the pig.

Above
Water buffalo are highly prized as funeral sacrifices; the piebald buffalo is considered the most valuable.

Right
An intricately carved, painted and decorated funerary shed houses the coffin of the deceased before it is taken to its final resting place. The roosters on the sun symbol stand for the east and sunrise, the source of life in Toraja belief.

Top
A guard wearing his boar-tooth necklace keeps vigil over the coffin.

Above
Riding on a bed of bamboo poles, the coffin is borne from the funeral ground to its cliffside destination.

Below
A drummer provides the beat for traditional dancers on Saumlaki in the Tanimbar islands. In the past, the people of this little-explored island traded sea products for gold sovereigns, which their talented smiths melted and hammered into heavy heirlooms. These, together with special cloths, became part of the bride price, and were handed down for generations.

Above
A Tanimbar Islander wearing a fine cloth turban. The Tanimbarese are a racial mixture of Papuan (New Guinea) and Malay. In the past, the men of Tanimbar used a mixture of lime and coconut to dye their hair a golden yellow.

Above
An atoll north of the Tanimbar Islands. Indonesia's Maluku Province is dotted with beautiful islands and coral reefs.

Right
A Ternatean man passes a nut to his tame parrot. Ternate and its sister island Tidore are two volcanic cones rising out of the Molucca Sea. Until the 16th century the location of these islands—the only place in the world where clove trees grew—was a mystery to the West.

Above

Dani warriors, their bodies glistening with pig grease and soot, prepare for mock battle in Irian Jaya's Baliem Valley. The Baliem, discovered by a U.S. explorer in 1938, is a mild, fertile valley tucked in the high cordillera of mountains that runs the length of the island of New Guinea. Until the 1960s, the Baliem Dani used no metal implements, and resolved their disputes in large-scale elaborate ritual wars.

Top

A mummified Dani ancestor at Jiwika, in the Baliem Valley. Although most of their dead were cremated, the Dani sometimes preserved the corpses of particularly powerful chiefs so that the spirit of the "Big Men" would be available to see to the community's supernatural needs. The bodies were preserved by smoking, giving them a jet-black color..

Above

A Dani woman has smeared herself in yellow clay in mourning for a lost relative. In the past, the death of a male sibling could have cost her a finger joint. Although this practice has ended, even today one sees old Dani women with missing fingers.

Far left
Seashells were a form of currency for the Dani. The cowrie shells and baler shells that make up this warrior's neck ornament were especially valuable. Since the Baliem valley was effectively cut off from the sea, it is not difficult to imagine how special such items—which passed through a convoluted trade pathway before reaching the highlands—must have appeared.

Near left
A charming little girl from the island of Numfor in Irian Jaya's Cenderawasih Bay. The people of Numfor and nearby Biak are racially distinct from the Papuans of New Guinea, with mixed Papuan and Malay features.

Bottom left
A Dani warrior poses with his hardwood spear, bow and quiver of arrows. The headdress this man wears is made from the skin of the largest terrestrial animal on the island—the cassowary bird.

Above
The Sudirman Range near Irian Jaya's highest mountain, 4,884-meter (16,020 ft) Puncak Jaya, is capped by permanent snowfields despite the tropical latitude. Although early European explorers sailing past the island had reported the snowfields, for centuries their claims were held in disbelief.

Above
The Dani hut is perfectly designed for the climate of the Baliem Valley, its thatched roof and sides retaining heat at night and staying cool in the day. The Dani are expert farmers, cultivating their staple sweet potato in carefully shaped mounds.

Right
Although Western dress and ways are now finding their way into Irian Jaya's interior, many Dani still prefer their penis sheaths to trousers. The gourds used for these are carefully tended by the men, and stones and other weights are attached to encourage the fruit to elongate and reach the desired shape. This man has also pierced his septum, which allows him to display a boar's tusk to advantage.

Overleaf
Two young boys have discovered the perfect way to cool off on eastern Biak Island.

"...it was certainly about the last aeroplane that I would have wished upon myself if returning to base in bad weather after losing an engine!"

CAPT ERIC 'WINKLE' BROWN CBE DSC AFC RN ON THE ME 410 - SEE PAGE 97

Zerstörergeschwader 1 (ZG 1) adopted a cartoon image of a Hornet for its Messerschmitt Me 410s. The nose of this Me 410B-2/U2/R4 bristles with armament. Standard fit on the 'B-2 was two 7.9mm machine-guns in the nose (gun ports visible in between the nose glazings) and two 20mm cannon either side of the nose (gun port below the Hornet's 'sting'). The U2/R4 modification put two more 20mms in the bomb bay (the doors of which are open) and another pair of 20mms in the pod under the centre section. For more on the Me 410, turn to page 66.

CONTENTS

Cover: A Focke-Wulf Fw 190A-8 of JG 26 Based In Belgium, July 1944 - see pages 58 and 64. Part of the Airfix D-Day 70th anniversary releases which included armoured fighting vehicles and warships.

These pages: floatplane Junkers Ju 52/3ms were used by the Luftwaffe for Operation MERKUR (Mercury), the invasion of Crete, May 1941. Airfix has produced a beautiful 1:72 kit of the 'Tante Ju' on floats, a Ju 52/3mg6e of Seetransportstaffel 1. With many thanks to Airfix **www.airfix.com**

SPOTLIGHTS

ABBREVIATIONS / GLOSSARY
To help readers, details of Luftwaffe ranks can be found in *Emil and Gustav* (page 6) and in *First of Many* (page 12) is a break-down of Luftwaffe unit structure and unit prefixes.

PREVIOUSLY PUBLISHED 2014
ISBN: 978 1 80282 767 5
Editor: Ken Ellis
Updates/corrections: Paul Hamblin
Senior editor, specials: Roger Mortimer
Email: roger.mortimer@keypublishing.com
Design: Steve Donovan and Mike Carr
Advertising Sales Manager: Brodie Baxter
Email: brodie.baxter@keypublishing.com
Tel: 01780 755131
Advertising Production: Debi McGowan
Email: debi.mcgowan@keypublishing.com

SUBSCRIPTION/MAIL ORDER
Key Publishing Ltd, PO Box 300, Stamford, Lincs, PE9 1NA
Tel: 01780 480404
Subscriptions email: subs@keypublishing.com
Mail Order email: orders@keypublishing.com
Website: www.keypublishing.com/shop

PUBLISHING
Group CEO and Publisher: Adrian Cox

Published by:
Key Publishing Ltd, PO Box 100, Stamford, Lincs, PE9 1XQ
Tel: 01780 755131
Website: www.keypublishing.com

PRINTING
Precision Colour Printing Ltd, Haldane, Halesfield 1, Telford, Shropshire. TF7 4QQ

DISTRIBUTION
Seymour Distribution Ltd, 2 Poultry Avenue, London, EC1A 9PU
Enquiries Line: 02074 294000.

We are unable to guarantee the bona fides of any of our advertisers. Readers are strongly recommended to take their own precautions before parting with any information or item of value, including, but not limited to money, manuscripts, photographs, or personal information in response to any advertisements within this publication.

EMIL
and Gustav

SAM TYLER EXAMINES THE PEDIGREE OF

A PAIR OF SURVIVING MESSERSCHMITT Bf 109s

Above
'Black Six' on a sortie from Duxford, shortly after it had arrived from Benson, 1991.
SGT RICK BREWELL – RAF PUBLIC RELATIONS

Stroll through the RAF Museum at Hendon and among hardware including Panavia Tornados, a prototype Eurofighter and a mock-up of the F-35 Joint Strike Fighter can be found a pair of their World War Two equivalents, a Messerschmitt Bf 109E and a 'G.

The E-model became widely known among its pilots and ground crew as the 'Emil'. Not surprisingly, when the improved Bf 109G came long, it was given the Teutonic name 'Gustav'.

The paths these two thoroughbreds took to Hendon included time with a specialist RAF unit operating a 'circus' of captured enemy machines.

FORCED DOWN AND RESURRECTED
Built at Leipzig by Erla Machinenwerk, Bf 109E-4 werke nummer 4101 was delivered to Jagdgeschwader (JG) 51, part of Luftflotte 2, at Pihen in Northern France on September 5, 1940. It

was modified in the field to fighter-bomber status and became *Black 12* of 2/JG 51, based at Wissant, near Calais.

On a fighter sweep over Kent on November 27, Lt Wolfgang Teumer came off worst in an encounter with Flt Lt George Christie DFC flying a Biggin Hill-based Spitfire. With hits in his radiator and his radio out of action, Teumer belly-landed the fighter at Manston – the Kent airfield became the final destination of a large number of Luftwaffe aircraft, either damaged or with their pilots confused as to where they were. (See the panel, page 8.)

The forlorn Bf 109E was taken to the huge dump of battered and twisted metal run by 49 Maintenance Unit (MU) at Faygate, Sussex. Thankfully it was quickly decided it would be better rebuilt for evaluation purposes.

'Emil' 4101 was issued to Rolls-Royce at Hucknall, Notts, on December 14, 1940, and many components from other Bf 109s

were used in its resurrection. Painted in RAF camouflage but with yellow undersides and given the serial DG200, it made its first flight under 'new management' on February 25, 1941. Rolls-Royce flew it 32 times, assessing the Daimler-Benz DB 601 engine's characteristics.

A well-known series of images of DG200 flying without a canopy come from this time. Rolls-Royce test pilot Harvey Hayworth was tall and could only fly the 'Emil' with the canopy removed. After Harvey, the remainder of DG200's flying life was without the luxury of a canopy!

SECOND CAREER
From Rolls-Royce, DG200 transferred to de Havilland at Hatfield, Herts, in February 1942 for propeller testing. Later that month it was at the Aeroplane & Armament Experimental Establishment at Boscombe Down, Wiltshire.

In April it joined 1426 (Enemy Aircraft) Flight at Duxford, near

Cambridge, where it was used to familiarise aircrew and 'ack-ack' gun crews with the shape and sound of the opposition. No.1426 moved to Collyweston, alongside Wittering, near Stamford, on April 12, 1943.

The 'Emil' was flown extensively, often transiting to Allied fighter units. For example a 'circus' tour in July and August 1942 with Heinkel He 111H AW177 and one of 1426's two Junkers Ju 88As visited the USAAF base at Atcham, Shropshire, before moving on to Heston and Northolt, west of London, and finally Boscombe Down.

By September 1943 it had been decided to retire this Battle of Britain veteran, and it went to Stafford for storage. In theory, DG200 was secured for 'museum use', but its future was by no means assured. Many types got as far as this only to fall victim to a purge

on space at an RAF station or to be wrongly identified and scrapped, or terminally damaged in transit.

The 'Emil' lived a charmed life, moving to Pengam Moors, Cardiff, during the summer of 1944 and then to Stanmore in Middlesex, Wroughton in Wiltshire and Fulbeck, Lincolnshire. Occasionally it was sent for display at special events, including duty at Horse Guards Parade in London for Battle of Britain week celebrations in the mid-1950s. By 1960 it was at Biggin Hill and 'wearing' a 'Galland' canopy from a Bf 109G.

By September 1969 the Bf 109E-4 was at St Athan in Wales and given a major restoration, including ➤

Above
'Black 12' on show inside the 'Battle of Britain Experience' at Hendon. KEN ELLIS

Left
Bf 109E DG200 flying without its 'hood', early 1941. ROLLS-ROYCE

Below
Restored as 'Black 12', Bf 109E 4101 following restoration at St Athan, circa 1976. KEC

"Rolls-Royce test pilot Harvey Hayworth was tall and could only fly the 'Emil' with the canopy removed."

ONE THAT GOT AWAY

It probably sank in while he was taxying, but by then Lt Horst Prenzel had run out of options. He had landed at Manston, Kent, an error that very probably increased his life expectancy. Surrendering, he had presented Britain with *White 6*, an Erla-built Bf 109G-6 of I/JG 301.

On July 27, 1944, six days after its arrival, the 'Gustav' was ferried to the Royal Aircraft Establishment at Farnborough in RAF markings and with the serial TP814. At the end of August TP814 joined the Air Fighting Development Unit at Wittering and was used in performance trials against a Mustang III and a Spitfire IX. Its RAF career came to an end on November 23, 1944 when it crashed on take-off. Its pilot was fine, but the fighter was declared a write-off.

Ground crew posing with 'Gustav' TP814 at Wittering, late 1944, during the fighter's brief period with the resident AFDU. SID CARTER VIA ALAN CURRY

the fitting of a mock-up 'Emil' canopy that had come from the set of the *Battle of Britain* film. It was installed in the Battle of Britain hall at Hendon in May 1978, a genuine veteran of the momentous aerial battle of 1940.

NICE KITE

Erla also built Bf 109G-2 10639, which on October 21, 1942 was issued to III/JG 77, becoming *Black 6* and beginning a long ferry to North Africa via Italy and Greece. Based initially at Bir el Abd in Egypt, the 'Gustav' became the personal mount of Lt Heinz Lüdemann.

During air combat on November 4, Lüdemann came off worst. Although injured he managed to bring *Black 6* down for a forced landing. The Messerschmitt was

taken to Gambut Main, near Tobruk, for repair. It was here that it was 'discovered' by personnel of 3 Squadron RAAF as they took over the airfield. Led by Sqn Ldr Bobby Gibbes DFC, the unit was equipped with Curtiss Kittyhawk Is and IIs.

Gibbes was determined to sample the Bf 109G and issued instructions that it be patched up and made airworthy. It was given RAF roundels and a fin flash and his personal codes, 'CV-V'. Gibbes flew *V-for-Victor* for the first time on November 15 and later wrote: "The '109 is a hell of a nice kite with terrific performance."

The Bf 109 was then flown frequently by a variety of pilots. Its last sortie in North Africa was very probably on February 24, 1943, when it was in mock combat with a Spitfire V.

TOURING 'CIRCUS'

Other eyes had focused on this 'rogue' Bf 109 and it was crated and shipped to Liverpool. A road convoy took the Luftwaffe fighter

"Reg Hallam strapped into *Tango-Victor* at Benson on March 17, 1991 – and a genuine Messerschmitt Bf 109 was once again flying in British skies."

to Collyweston where it was issued to 1426 (Enemy Aircraft) Flight on November 26, 1943. At this point, 'Emil' 4101 had been packed off to storage at Stafford, postponing its first association with 'Gustav' 10639 by a couple of months.

Once the Bf 109G was unpacked it was clear much work was needed to get it operational. With the RAF serial RN228 painted on the tail, it had its first flight in Britain on February 19, 1944. As well as touring 'circus' detachments, RN228 was also employed in comparative trials with Allied fighters at the Air Fighting Development Unit at Wittering, just a mile away to the east.

With the work of 1426 Flight wound down, RN228 was ferried to Tangmere, Sussex, to join the Enemy Aircraft Flight of the Central Fighter Establishment. Its stay on the south coast came to an end when the 'Gustav' was sent to 47 MU at Sealand, near Chester, for packing into a storage crate.

Like DG200, the Bf 109G was moved around a variety of storage sites: Wroughton, Stanmore Park, Fulbeck and then Cranwell, Lincs. During this time, both Messerschmitts would have shared hangar space. The 'Gustav' was a regular attendee at the annual Horse Guards Parade static display from 1949 to 1955 – and DG200 is known to have attended in 1954 and 1955, very likely the pair's first appearance in public together.

BACK IN THE AIR

In September 1961 a scheme was hatched to return the 'Gustav' to flying condition and it was moved to the fighter station at Wattisham, Suffolk. The project foundered, but it had been drawn to the attention of Russ Snadden, a patient and determined restorer. On September 30, 1972, the Messerschmitt was airborne again – well, as cargo inside two RAF Hercules flying from Wattisham to Lyneham, Wiltshire.

RAF life being as it is, Russ and his dedicated team had to change 'workshops' several times, moving to Northolt in July 1975 and to Benson in Oxfordshire in July 1983. The Daimler-Benz DB 605A engine fired into life for the first time on July 8, 1990. An exceptional restoration project was reaching its climax.

Technically it was an RAF Museum airframe, but the museum was not in a position to become an 'operator'. So a unique co-operation between Hendon and the Imperial War Museum at Duxford began – and on October 26, 1990, the very apt civil registration G-USTV was allocated. It would operate on a Permit to Fly basis and, at some point in its future, be returned to the RAF Museum.

Reg Hallam flew *Tango-Victor* at Benson on March 17, 1991 – and a genuine Bf 109 was once again flying in British skies. (The 1969 film *Battle of Britain* had introduced the Rolls-Royce Merlin 500-powered Hispano Buchón to the world of 'warbirds' –

see page 10.) It was ferried to its new base at Duxford on July 12.

The decision had been made to retire the Bf 109G at the end of the 1997 flying season and October 12 was scheduled to be *Tango-Victor*'s last flight. During the display the fighter was seen to be trailing white vapour and air traffic let the pilot know. He elected to abort the routine and effect a landing, the 'Gustav' settling into an easterly approach to the grass strip. High and fast, the Messerschmitt touched down, but application of the brakes would have resulted in a violent nose-over.

The pilot took off again, flew over the M11 and made a tail-down landing in a farm field to the east. All was well until the Bf 109 came to a ploughed section and tipped over, ending up inverted. The pilot was unhurt, but temporarily trapped. Six years of delighting audiences had come to a sad ending. 'Gustav' was restored to static condition and on March 10, 2002, was reunited with 'Emil' at Hendon. ☒

LUFTWAFFE HIERARCHY

Luftwaffe ranks		Abbreviations	RAF equivalents
Oberst		Oberst	Group Captain
Oberstleutnant		ObstIt	Wing Commander
Major		Major	Squadron Leader
Hauptmann		Hptm	Flight Lieutentant
Oberleutnant		Oblt	Flying Officer
Leutnant		Lt	Pilot Officer
Oberfaehnrich		Ofhr	Officer aspirant, junior officer under training
Stabsfeldwebel		Stabfw	Warrant Officer
Oberfeldwebel		Obfw	Flight Sergeant
Feldwebel		Fw	Sergeant
Unterfeldwebel		Ufw	None
Unteroffizier		Uffz	Corporal
Hauptgefreiter		Hptf	None
Obergefreiter		Obgf	Leading Aircraftman
Gefreiter		Gf	Aircraftman, 1st Class
Flieger		Fg	Aircraftman, 2nd Class

Left
'Black Six' inside Hendon's 'Milestones of Flight' hall.
KEY-DUNCAN CUBITT

MESSERSCHMITT
Bf 109

WHY Bf 109 AND NOT Me 109?

A Bf 109B-1, produced at the BFW works at Augsburg in 1937. Powered by a Junkers Jumo 210, 'B-1s were fitted with two-blade propellers and, with the exception of the very early examples, featured a cropped spinner. *KEY COLLECTION*

Many readers query the designation Bf 109, and insist that it is the Me 109. Colloquially the fighter was referred to as the 'Me 109' through the war – and beyond – but officially this was never the case. Willy Messerschmitt's Messerschmitt Flugzeugbau merged with the Bayerische Flugzeugwerke (BFW) in September 1927, the latter company offering greater potential for investment and all-metal construction. The advent of the Bf 109 changed the company's prospects beyond anyone's wildest dreams – it became Germany's largest aircraft manufacturer of the war – and in July 1938 BFW was renamed as Messerschmitt AG to reflect this.

The Reichsluftfahrtministerium (RLM - German Air Ministry) abbreviated BFW to Bf, and the Bf 108 Taifun (Typhoon) was the first to appear. Then follows the Bf 109, Bf 110 and the Bf 161 - Bf 162 twin-engined fighters brought the 'Bf' designations to an end. The first 'Me' was the rocket-propelled Komet, the Me 163.

Right
Centrepiece of the Imperial War Museum Duxford's Battle of Britain exhibition is Erla-built Bf 109E-3 1190 'White 4' of 4/ JG 26. On September 30, 1940 Uffz Perez was flying 'White 4' on bomber escort when he was engaged in air combat over the Sussex coast. His engine failed and he made a forced landing near Eastbourne; he was unhurt and captured.
KEY-DUNCAN CUBITT

Right centre
A Bf 109B-2 of the Condor Legion's Jagdgruppe 88 (J/88) in Spain 1937-1938.

Messerschmitt Bf 109E-4 'Yellow 2' of II/JG 27, 1940. PETE WEST © 2014

MESSERSCHMITT Bf 109E-3

Construction: Just how many Bf 109s were built is a hotly-debated subject, suffice it to say a figure of around 35,000 is generally accepted, including more than 4,000 Bf 109Es. In Germany they were also built by Arado, Erla Maschinewerk, Fieseler, Focke-Wulf. Wiener Neustädter Flugzeugwerke built them in Austria and about 600 were produced in Hungary. In Czechoslovakia, the Bf 109 was built by Avia as the S-99 with DB 605s and the S-199 with Jumo 211Fs post-war. In Spain, Hispano built the Bf 109 post-war as the Ha 1109 with Hispano-Suiza engines and finally the Ha 1112 Buchón powered by Rolls-Royce Merlin 500-45s.

First flight: The prototype, the Bf 109 V1, made its first flight on May 29, 1935 powered by a Rolls-Royce Kestrel V as the intended Junkers Jumo 201A was unavailable. The V2, with a Jumo 201A, followed in January 1936. The Bf 109D series was the first to introduce Daimler-Benz engines.

Powerplant: One 1,175hp (876kW) Daimler-Benz DB 601A 12-cylinder inverted 'vee' piston engine.

Dimensions: Span 32ft 4¹/₂in (9.86m) Length 28ft 4¹/₄in (8.64m) Height 8ft 2¹/₄in (2.49m) Wing area 176ft² (16.35m²).

Weights: Empty 4,189lb (1,900kg) Loaded 5,875lb (2,664kg).

Performance: Max speed 348mph (560km/h) at 14,560ft (4,440m) Service ceiling 34,450ft (10,500m) Max range 410 miles (660km).

Armament: Two 7.9mm machine-guns in upper cowling, one 20mm firing through the propeller hub, two 20mm in the wings.

"When dived and then pulled up into a climb there was little to choose between the US and German fighter ....but the Mustang could steadily out-dive the Bf 109G-6 and had no difficulty in out-turning the Messerschmitt."

CAPTAIN ERIC 'WINKLE' BROWN - SEE PAGE 97

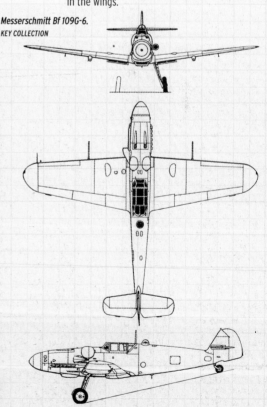

Messerschmitt Bf 109G-6.
KEY COLLECTION

Historic Flying's Hispano Buchón 'Yellow 10', looking very much the part at its Duxford base. Built by Hispano post-war and powered by a Rolls-Royce Merlin 500, it is panted in the colours that it wore while flying for the 1969 film 'Battle of Britain'. Around a dozen Bf 109s are airworthy, the bulk being Buchóns. Of the original Bf 109s about 15 'Emils' survive, a dozen and upwards of 30 Bf 109Fs and 'Gs, plus a handful of Avia-built examples. COL POPE

FIRST
of many

ANDREW THOMAS RELATES THE STORY BEHIND A BATTERED JU 88 FIN TIP THAT SITS ON HIS DESK

Above
Hptn Karl Rohloff's crew of 9/KG 4 flew a Ju 88A similar to this on their final fateful sortie on July 8, 1940. VIA JOHN WEAL

Right
The first attack on the Ju 88 was made by Fg Off Tony Lovell, on the right. VIA C F SHORES

After success in Norway and during the Blitzkrieg that ran through the Low Countries and France, Kampfgeschwader 4's III Gruppe got ready for its greatest test yet. The day after France surrendered, June 22, 1940, the unit's Junkers Ju 88s settled in to Schiphol, Amsterdam.

Gruppenkommandeur, Major Erich Bloedorn, prepared his men for operations against Britain. In the weeks before the sustained assault began, Luftwaffe bombers mounted small-scale attacks to probe the defences and laid mines around the British coast in to interdict coastal shipping.

With what Churchill described as the Battle of Britain about to begin, the bulk of the RAF's fighter defences were concentrated under 11 and 12 Groups in southern England and the Midlands. Significant elements were based in the north under 13 Group to protect east coast ports and naval bases on the Firth of Forth and in the Orkneys. North Yorkshire was the dividing line between 13 Group and its more southerly cohorts.

KAMPFGESCHWADER 4

The badge of KG 4 'General Wever', a white shuttle on a red shield taken from the Wever family coat of arms.

Formed out of KG 253 and equipped with He 111Ps, KG4 was named after General Walter Wever, the leading proponent of a strategic Luftwaffe bomber force who was killed in 1936.

KG 4's III Gruppe was formed at Nordhausen under Major Evers on May 1, 1939. It controlled three Staffeln:, 7/KG 4, 8/KG 4 and 9/KG 4. During February 1940, part of the Gruppe began conversion to the Junkers Ju 88A-1, the best bomber available to the Luftwaffe at that time. These were used during the assault against Norway in April. After the fall of Norway, the Gruppe returned to Germany, re-establishing at Delmenhorst from where it participated in the Blitzkrieg against France and the Low Countries that opened on May 10.

Returning to Germany to fully convert to the Ju 88, III/KG 4 was briefly based at Antwerp's Deurne airfield before it settled at Schiphol, Amsterdam, on June 23, with a strength of 35 Ju 88s.

Among 13 Group's units was 41 Squadron, based at Catterick in Yorkshire and flying Spitfires under 32-year-old Sqn Ldr H R L 'Robin' Hood, a former cadet from the RAF College, Cranwell. A little further south at Church Fenton, was the recently-formed, Hurricane-equipped 249 Squadron, part of 12 Group and led by Sqn Ldr John Grandy – aged 28 and a future Chief of the Air Staff.

Under Grandy's dynamic leadership 249 had worked up intensively at Leconfield, near Beverley, and was the first unit to achieve 1,000 hours flying in a month while training.

FOREWARNED
Early in the morning of July 8, Hauptman Karl Rohloff, Staffelkapitän of 9/KG 4, prepared his crew for a mission out of Schiphol. They were to cross the North Sea on an armed reconnaissance along the east coast, looking for coastal shipping to report and attack.

The rest of the crew comprised flight engineer Unteroffiziers Heinz Oechler, wireless operator Artur Kühnapfel and gunner George Abel. Oechler and Kühnapfel had been flying together for four years, initially on Ju 52s and then on Heinkel He 111s, throughout the Polish, Norwegian and French campaigns. They joined 9/KG 4 at Schiphol.

The four Germans climbed aboard Ju 88A-1 3094 '5J+AT' and headed west over the North Sea towards Sunderland. At about 11:30 they were off the Yorkshire coast flying intermittently in cloud at 15,000ft (4,572m) when a convoy was spotted, heading north. The ➤

Above left
Catterick's hangars provide a backdrop to a Spitfire I of 41 Squadron at it is prepared for flight by Plt Off Webster early in the war. J T WEBSTER

LUFTWAFFE **UNIT STRUCTURE**

Staffel

Plural - Staffeln. Smallest combat flying unit, normally of nine aircraft. Denoted using Arabic numerals. RAF equivalent would be a Squadron.

Gruppe

Plural - Gruppen. Comprising three (in later years four) Staffeln plus a Stab, headquarters, or staff, flight. Denoted using Roman numerals, eg I, II, III. Thus 3/JG 20 would be the 3rd Staffeln of Jagdgeschwader 20. RAF equivalent would be a Wing.

Geschwader

Plural - Geschwadern. Comprising three (in later years four) Gruppen plus a Stab, headquarters, or staff, flight. Denoted using Arabic numerals, eg 1, 2, 3. Thus I/JG 20 would be the 1st Gruppen of Jagdgeschwader 20 and Stab/JG 20 would be its headquarters flight. Geschwader were usual given a prefix relating to their role - see the other table for a decode. RAF equivalent would be a Group.

Note: To use the full designation, I/JG 20 *should* be presented as I./JG 20, as a full stop behind a number in German is the equivalent of 1st in English. To keep things simple, these full stops have not been included in this publication.

crew would doubtless have prepared a sighting report before going in to attack.

Unknown to them, they would have been detected by one of the then secret Chain Home radio direction finding (radar) stations. At the Junkers' height, the radar coverage extended well out to sea.

CALLED TO INTERCEPT

From Catterick, two Spitfires of 41 Squadron, Mk.I P9429 flown by Fg Off Tony Lovell, and his No.2, Sgt Jack Allison, had been vectored toward the intruder. They spotted Rohloff's aircraft off Scarborough and promptly swept in to attack.

In their first pass 0.303in bullets riddled the bomber, putting the starboard engine out of action and also hitting the cockpit, wounding Abel, the gunner. Rohloff managed to evade the Spitfires but his Junkers had been badly hit. Probably realising that it would not make it back to Holland he jettisoned the four 551lb (250kg) bombs and turned towards land.

Airborne from Church Fenton were the three Hurricanes of 249 Squadron.

This was Green Section led by Fg Off Denis Parnall in P3615, with Plt Off Hugh 'Beazle' Beazley in P3055 as No.2, and Sgt Alistair Main in P2995 as No.3.

The crippled bomber was about 15 miles (24km) north of Flamborough Head and heading south when Green Section spotted it, and as Parnall was setting up the Hurricanes for an attack he saw the Spitfires breaking away. Rohloff desperately evaded by flying slowly and executing several stall turns.

In his report, Parnall noted: "I fired a nine-seconds burst, commencing at 350 yards, breaking away at 40 yards." He did not note any return fire before Beazley followed him in.

Beazley wrote: "After a two-second burst, [the] enemy stall-turned to right and I had to go into firm pitch to pull up and follow him round. Enemy entered cloud but I caught him coming out the other side and got in a burst before he again turned sharply to the left, diving slightly.

"I again opened fire as he straightened out. I observed white streaks coming past the starboard wing. I ceased firing as he dived into cloud again." Beazley did not see the Junkers again, but he noted a strong smell of burning metal as the Hurricane entered cloud.

Although it had become enveloped in cloud, Rohloff's crippled Junkers gained little respite. It was Alastair Main's turn: "I gave a short burst before No.2 broke away. Following the

> ## "I again opened fire as he straightened out. I observed white streaks coming past the starboard wing. I ceased firing as he dived into cloud again."

LUFTWAFFE TERMINOLOGY

Unit prefixes	Abbreviation	Role
Aufklärungs	Auflk	Tactical reconnaissance
Fernaufklärungs	Fern	Long-range, or strategic, reconnaissance
Jagd	J	Fighter
Jagdbomber	Jabo	Fighter-bomber
Kampf	K	Bomber
Küstenflieger	Kü Fl	Coastal aviation, Navy co-operation
Nachtjagd	NJ	Night-fighter
Panzer	Pz	Anti-tank
Schlacht	SG	Close support
Schnellkampf	SK	High-speed bomber
Sturm	Sturm	Assault, usual in terms of fighters engaging bomber streams
Sturzkampf	Stuka	Dive-bomber
Zerstörer	Z	Heavy fighter (ie twin-engined)

Note: So, a geschwader operating Messerschmitt Bf 110s was a Zerstörergeschwader, abbreviated as ZG; a geschwader flying Focke-Wulf Fw 190s was a Jagdgeschwader, abbreviated as JG, and so on.

wife, Eveline Cardwell. Although unarmed, she was undaunted, and as the injured German airman approached she beckoned him to raise his arms. When he did so, she took his pistol, before sending a farm worker to summon the Local Defence Volunteers (later known as the Home Guard). He and his two colleagues were taken into captivity and remained as prisoners of war for the duration.

The hulk of '5J+AT' was located and two machine-guns recovered, together with some of the wreckage. Kurt Rohloff's remains were buried with full military ▷

enemy aircraft through cloud I came out to find myself on his tail, gave a burst of three to four seconds."

TAKE TO THE SILK

By this time both of the Junkers' engines were on fire and Main broke off to re-join the rest of the section. Struggling to retain control of the doomed Junkers, Rohloff ordered his crew to bale out. No sooner had they exited than control was lost and the aircraft crashed and exploded close to the seaside town of Hornsea with its

gallant pilot still aboard.

It was 11:42 and 249 Squadron had achieved a victory in its first combat. This was to be followed by another 327½ aircraft claim as destroyed. With 109 'probables' and 242 damaged, this tally made 249 one of the RAF's top scoring fighter squadrons.

One of the Germans (exactly which of three survivors it has been impossible to identify) landed in a field at East Carlton Farm where he was spotted by farmer's

The fin of '5T+AT' in the field where it came down on July 8.
VIA MARK POSTLETHWAITE

Right
The tip of a propeller blade of '5J+AT' that survives to this day.
AUTHOR

Below
The shattered remains of Karl Rohloff's Ju 88, near the village of Aldbrough in East Yorkshire.
VIA MARK POSTLETHWAITE

PLUCK AND PRESENCE OF MIND

Twenty-one-year-old Tony Lovell went on to have a highly successful flying career. A committed Christian, he is one of the least known RAF 'aces', but ended the war as Wg Cdr Tony Lovell DSO* DFC*. He led a Wing in the Mediterranean and gaining 22 victories, six of them shared. He died in a flying accident shortly after the end of the war.

His wingman, Londoner Jack Allison, served later in the summer in 611 and 92 Squadrons, shooting down a Bf 109 while with 92. Commissioned in 1941, he was killed in a flying accident in 1942.

Alistair Main survived barely a week, killed when Hurricane P2995's Merlin cut as he was taking off from Church Fenton. He hit wires before crashing into a wood near Copmanthorpe.

For both Parnall and Beazley, the share in the destruction of Rohloff's Ju 88 was their first success. Parnall flew with 249 through the Battle of Britain claiming a further four victories (three shared), but on September 18 his Hurricane was shot down and the 25-year old was killed.

Hugh Beazley, an Oxford history graduate, also flew through the Battle, seeing much action, and in 1941 moved with the Squadron to Malta. There he took his final tally to two and four shared victories. He ended the war as a Wing Commander and passed away on June 13, 2011.

For her part in capturing an armed German airman, Eveline Cardwell was awarded the British Empire Medal which was presented to her by the King at Hornsea on August 1. The citation noted her: "great pluck and presence of mind".

Winston Churchill commented glowingly on Mrs Cardwell's actions, while the incident is also thought to have been the inspiration for a scene in the 1942 film *Mrs Miniver*, starring Greer Garson and Walter Pidgeon, that won six Academy awards.

DESK TOP SURVIVOR

When the wreckage of '5J+AT' was examined, the front of the fuselage had been destroyed in the crash but large parts of the wings and the rear fuselage, including the fin, were mostly intact. Part of the fin with the swastika painted on it was claimed by 249 Squadron as a trophy; but subsequently, during various unit moves, it went missing.

The tip of one of the propeller blades, with a bullet hole punched through it, was neatly sawn off and kept locally. The words 'Junkers 88, Aldborough, Yorks, July 8, 1940' were engraved upon it.

During the late 1960s it was given to North Lincolnshire businessman and aviation historian, Peter Green, becoming part of his archive. Last year he generously gifted it to the author, providing the catalyst to this feature. This small but interesting relic of those dark days of 1940 sits next to the keyboard as these words are typed. ✚

honours and after the war his body was re-interred in the German cemetery at Cannock Chase in Staffordshire.

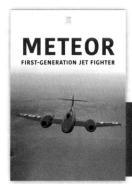

JUNKERS *Ju 88*

A Junkers Ju 88A-4 of KG 1. *PETE WEST © 2014*

UNDER **OTHER FLAGS**

Wright Patterson's Ju 88D-1/Trop in 1988, shortly after its restoration to Romanian colours was completed. KEY-DUNCAN CUBITT

The markings on the Ju 88 didn't look right as it taxied in to surrender at Limassol on Cyprus on July 23, 1943. The defecting pilot was Romanian, and so was his Ju 88D-1, both having escaped from a base in the Ukraine. It was ferried to the USA arriving at Wright Field, Ohio, in October. Here it was evaluated until 1946 when it was put into storage in Arizona. It returned to Wright in 1960 to join what is now the National Museum of the USAF. After a painstaking restoration, it was returned to its Romanian colours in 1988.

Romania joined the Axis powers in November 1940 and by the following June took a limited role in Operation BARBAROSSA, the invasion of the USSR. As a vital source of oil to the Third Reich, Romania was frequently targeted by Allied bombers. In 1944 the Soviet Union returned the compliment and invaded Romania; the country joining the Allies for the remainder of the war.

Inside the Battle of Britain Experience at the RAF Museum, Hendon, is Ju 88R-1 360043, which has been on site since August 1978. This is another example of a defector, touching down at Dyce, near Aberdeen, on May 9, 1943. The Ju 88 was sent to Farnborough for trials of its FuG 202 Liechtenstein radar - see opposite - after which it was issued to 1426 (Enemy Aircraft) Flight at Collyweston, Northants, to familiarise Allied pilots on the recognition points of the opposition. There are about a dozen surviving Ju 88s, the largest population having been salvaged from where they fell in Norway. KEY-DUNCAN CUBITT

A torpedo-armed Ju 88A-14 of KG 77, southern France, 1944.

JUNKERS Ju 88

Construction:	Junkers and sub-contractors built 14,980 of all models, including 7,000-plus 'A variants. A large number of sub-variants, for heavy fighter, night-fighter, long-range recce, torpedo attack and ground attack.
First Flight:	December 21, 1936, by prototype Ju 88 V1 D-AQEN.
Powerplants:	Two 1,340hp (999kW) Junkers Jumo 211 12-cylinder radials.
Dimensions:	Span 65ft 7½in (20.0m) Length 47ft 2in (14.37m) Height 15ft 11in (15.91m) Wing area 586ft² (54.43m²).
Weights:	Empty 21,737lb (9,859kg) Max loaded 30,865lb (14,000kg).
Performance:	Max speed 292mph (469km/h) at 17,390ft (5,300m). Range 1,112 miles (1,789km). Service ceiling 26,900ft (8,199m).
Armament:	Four 7.9mm machine-guns; one in the nose, one in a ventral 'gondola', two in the rear cockpit. Up to 2,210lb (1,002kg) of bombs externally and up to 4,420lb (2,004kg) of bombs internally.
Crew:	Four: pilot, navigator/bomb-aimer, radio operator/gunner and rear gunner.

Junkers Ju 88G-7a night-fighter with FuG 220 Lichtenstein SN-2 radar aerial arrays and two 20mm upward-firing 'Schräge Musik' cannon.
KEY COLLECTION

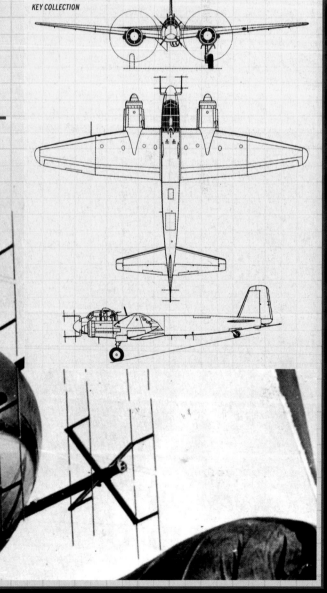

> **"The experience of performing a dive-bombing attack with a machine the size of the Ju 88 was something more than awe-inspiring. But the aircraft handled so beautifully that one did not have to be particularly intrepid..."**

CAPTAIN ERIC 'WINKLE' BROWN - SEE PAGE 97

A close-up of the nose of the RAF Museum's Ju 88R-1 when it arrived in Britain in May 1943.

UNINVITED
Visitors

BILL NORMAN RECOUNTS AN INCIDENT WHEN DRAMA DESCENDED ON A YORKSHIRE FARM

Clockwise from right
Matt Young, quick-acting Lewis gunner, 1940.

Matt Young's commendation.
BOTH VIA MATT YOUNG

Ju 88 '5J+ER' under guard at Dugglebly, October 1940.
NORTHERN ECHO

During the fifty or so years he farmed Manor Farm at Duggleby, near Malton, Jack Clarke had many visitors. Easily the most memorable were four strangers who dropped in one evening in 1940.

In the late afternoon and early evening of October 27, German aircraft launched a series of attacks on airfields in East Anglia, Lancashire and Yorkshire. A number of the latter were in the Malton area: Catfoss, Driffield, Leconfield and Linton-on-Ouse.

The streets of Beverley were machine-gunned at 18:10 hours and three people suffered slight wounds in North Bar. Leconfield was hit eight minutes later but suffered only minor damage, although a Polish airman is thought to have been seriously injured.

At 18:00 three Junkers Ju 88s had raided Driffield at low level, but caused no casualties and hardly any damage. One bomb exploded on the Kellythorpe road, alongside the airfield, making a crater 20ft (6m) deep and rupturing a water main.

OUT OF THE HAZE

Seconds after the raid on Driffield, two of the bombers flew northwards and passed close to a searchlight site of 4 Troop, 411 Battery, 54 Searchlight Regiment, Royal Artillery. This was alongside the A166 road at Fimber Field Farm, between the villages of Fridaythorpe and Wetwang.

Stockton-born Matt Young was a Lewis gunner with 'D' Section, 411 Battery, and it was his job to defend the searchlight site. On a clear day,

from their raised position on the wolds, the men at Fimber could see Driffield. But in the early evening of October 27 it was masked by haze.

Matt recalled: "Sgt Fraser had just arrived with the ration wagon. He was on site when we heard the bombs dropping at Driffield aerodrome. I immediately went to the gun position and we got orders from HQ at Huttons Ambo that we could engage the enemy – but at first we couldn't see anything."

Two Ju 88s in loose formation gradually emerged from the haze at low level. Matt remembered the bombers "flew in almost a straight line from Driffield: up the hillside" towards the searchlight position. As they drew near, Matt felt the urge to shoot but Fraser refused permission on the grounds that they might fire back. He made Matt wait for a safer opportunity.

"Just before they reached us, they started to bank to starboard, as if making for the coast. When they were about halfway round, Fraser let me fire. I set the gun going, followed my tracers and the ➤

> SECRET.

The Officer Commanding,
No.4. Troop. 411 Battery.

  I am to advise you that the A.A.Command have admitted the following claim :-
  Category 1 27th Oct. 40. 1 Aircraft by 411 Bty shared by 38 Lt.A.A.
  (Destroyed).   Regt., Driffield.

  Category 1 is that category in which all enemy aircraft known to be destroyed are placed. The detachment concerned is, of course No.4/5, Detachment Commander 4446794 L/Sgt Moody A.
  I wish to convey my congratulations to all concerned in this excellent achievement and in particular to congratulate 4453740 Gnr Young M who was No.1. on the gun.
  I am particularly impressed by the fact that your No.4/5 Detachment had thought out and selected in advance the man judged most suitable to act as No.1. on the gun in the event of attack by low flying enemy aircraft, and it is good to know that such forethought has been rewarded.
  Sgt. Fraser's command of the situation was, as was well to be expected, of the highest order and No.2. on the gun No 4453898 Gnr Crowe A.H. also deserves special mention.
  I enclose sufficient copies of this letter for you to issue personally to the men concerned.
  Copies of this letter have also been sent to O.C.s. All Troops who should arrange to circulate such copies round their Detachments.

Hutton Hall,
Malton.   Captain,
7.11.40.   Commanding 411 Bty.,
      54th Searchlight Regiment R.A.,T.A.

No.4.Troop 5 copies.
Nos.1,2&3 Troops 1 copy each.
File 1 copy.

"I set the gun going, followed my tracers and the full pan of 47 rounds into the port engine of the one nearest me."

Above
Jack Clarke at Manor Farm in 1990. BILL NORMAN

"It was very low; no more than 30ft above the ground," said. Jack. He could see a crash was inevitable; would the raider come to earth on his farm buildings or on the open land beyond?

The pilot was probably thinking along similar lines and could have been bracing himself for the worst. Fate was kind: the Junkers skimmed over Clarke's Dutch barn, narrowly missed the chimney pots of a house behind and bellied into the field that rises to the ancient barrow of Duggleby Howe. It gouged its way to the top of the rise, coming to rest alongside a hedge.

These were the last moments of Junkers Ju 88A-5 6129 '5J+ER' of

REMEMBRANCE AT CANNOCK

Flight engineer Oskar Piontek shares a grave in the German War Cemetery at Cannock Chase: Feldwebel Willi Meyer was a crewmember of Focke-Wulf Fw 200 Condor 'F8+EH' of I/KG 40, shot down by anti-aircraft fire on July 19, 1940 while mine-laying between Hartlepool and Crimdon Dean. BILL NORMAN

full pan of 47 rounds into the port engine of the one nearest me. They got round with their tails towards us and I put on another pan and fired again, but I don't know if it did any good. They didn't fire back, anyway."

As the bombers disappeared eastwards into the haze, Matt began to think he had caused no damage as both seemed to be getting safely away. However, "people at Fridaythorpe, who had been watching all the time, said that after I had finished firing and the planes were going back towards the coast the one I'd hit veered off."

UNWANTED ARRIVAL
Shortly after 18:00, Jack Clarke was busy shutting up the poultry huts in his fields at Manor Farm when he heard the laboured sounds of an aircraft approaching from the direction of North Grimston. Seconds later, he saw a crippled German bomber barely scrape over Duggleby Plum, the rising land to the north of the village, before settling even lower.

As it lurched towards Jack and the farm buildings 200 yards (182m) behind him, the Ju 88's flight path was marked by the debris of equipment discarded by the crew in an effort to lighten the load and gain more lift. With the port engine out and starboard impaired, this was to no avail. The Junkers staggered over the farmer's head.

7/KG 4. Its crew was Oberleutnant Friedrich Franz Podbielski (pilot), Unteroffiziers Hans Heier (observer), Karl von Kidrowski (wireless operator) and Oskar Piontek (flight engineer).

FRIEND AND FOE
Jack set off up the hill, but he soon found he was not alone. "Six of us scrambled up the hill towards it – myself, 'Josh' Jeffles, Bill Jeffles, Harold Hodgson, Ben Midgeley and John Gray. As we approached, three of the crew started walking towards us, hands raised in surrender.

"When we got within 20 yards of

them, one started to gesture with his hands – repeatedly raising them to elbow level. We stopped. He persisted in doing this and after a few moments set off back towards the plane.

"A number of us knew of the practice of crashed crews destroying their aircraft to prevent them falling into enemy hands. So when one of the Jeffles' boys shouted 'Hey up, he's going to blow her up!' there was a mad scramble back down the hill. Until then, I had thought I could run fast, but I was the last one down to the bottom!"

There was no explosion. When the would-be helpers realised it was not the crew's intention to 'fire' their aircraft, they cautiously returned. It was then that they realised the significance of the earlier gesture: the fourth crewman, Oskar Piontek, the only casualty, was pinned under the tail. His colleagues had been gesturing for help.

Whether Piontek had panicked and jumped out as the Ju 88 skidded across the field or had been thrown out on impact was not clear. Jack explained: "It did seem the human thing to do to help free him." In a spontaneous demonstration of the irony of war, friend and foe alike joined together to lift the tail unit and help a fellow in distress.

Using an overcoat as a makeshift stretcher they carried the injured man to Jack's farm. Placing Piontek on the kitchen table, Mrs Clarke got a pillow while his colleagues removed his boots and gloves and tried to make him as comfortable as possible.

Things did not look good for the Luftwaffe flight engineer, as Jack recalled. Piontek "was as good as dead even then. There was not a sound from him. He was very badly injured and had a gaping hole in his left side, presumably where the plane had been resting on him."

Members of the locally-billeted Manchester Regiment arrived with fixed bayonets and "took a very military stance" forcing the Germans to strip to the waist to ensure they concealed no weapons. It was a gesture some of those present felt to be: "unnecessary and rather ridiculous, for the prisoners were totally harmless. None of them gave any trouble".

Podbielski was taken to York, the rest to Driffield, where Oskar Piontek died of his injuries on November 15. He lies in the German war cemetery at Cannock Chase, Staffordshire.

"The plane was very low. If I'd had a stick long enough, I could've touched it. Its left engine was on fire and the plane had to rise to get over the trees."

WHY NO BOOTS?

During those wartime days, most people were souvenir hunters. Jack Clarke was no exception. When I spoke to him in the early 1990s, he recalled having been very impressed by the quality of the clothing worn by the fliers, so when the 'Manchesters' left behind Piontek's knee-length fur-lined flying boots and black kid-gloves, Jack resolved "to take care of them".

The boots were not in his charge for long. A couple of visits by Sgt Huddleston of the Driffield Constabulary, who confessed to being "totally unable to understand why this fellow had been flying in bare feet" were enough to ensure the boots were 'found' and duly handed over. The gloves were never mentioned by the sergeant and they served their new owner for many years after the war had ended.

TWIST IN THE TALE

Although there seemed no doubt that the demise of the Junkers was attributable to Matt Young, it was three days before he was allowed to visit the wreck. After he had submitted his report, he was confined to the Fimber site until he had been questioned by 'big wigs'. Apparently, a detachment of the 38th Light Anti-Aircraft Regiment, employed in the defence of Driffield, had also claimed the Junkers, so there had to be an inquiry.

Matt told the author it was "decided that I had to share it with the 38th, but I still don't know why." Both 411 Battery and Matt Young received commendations from Command HQ.

There is a twist to this tale. This particular Ju 88 had been ordered to attack Linton-on-Ouse, not Driffield. Hans Heier firmly believes Linton was the target they bombed. Certainly, three Ju 88s struck at Linton that evening, at about the same time as the raid on Driffield.

When one of the Junkers made a low-level strafing run over Linton it was, according to the station's Operations Record Book, given "such a hot reception that it veered off to the north and may have been the one that was brought down afterwards".

When I first researched this incident for publication in my 1993 book *Luftwaffe over the North* a number of eyewitnesses stated they had seen the 'Duggleby' Junkers in difficulties over the villages of Wharram-le-Street, North Grimston and Settrington shortly before it crashed. The crippled bomber's flight across these villages fitted comfortably with Matt Young's account.

In August 1998, 70-year-old John Wilson, of Slingsby, contacted me with an account that shed more

light on the incident. In October 1940, he was living at North Ings Farm, between Terrington and Sheriff Hutton, where there was a searchlight site.

John recalled that, in the late afternoon of October 27, he saw three German aeroplanes going over and heading towards Easingwold. "They weren't very high. Later, about five o'clock, one came back.

"The plane was very low. If I'd had a stick long enough, I could've touched it. Its left engine was on fire and the plane had to rise to get over the trees. As I recall, the right-hand engine had stopped and the left one was still going – but it was on fire. I told the men it was a German, but they didn't believe me. It flew over Terrington and towards Malton. Then we heard that it crashed at Duggleby." Despite this testament, the gunners at Linton were not given a 'share' in the Junkers 'kill'.

John Wilson's account puts the flight path of the crippled Ju 88 further west – nearer to Linton but still in line with North Grimston and Settrington. This increases the likelihood it was damaged over Linton-on-Ouse and passed nowhere near Fimber Field Farm. An element of doubt still remains but it does seem Matt Young's 'victim' might have got away with it. ☩

Above
A Lewis gun crew of 4 Troop, 411 Battery, at Weston Grange, near Malton. DAVID EVANS

RICHTHOFEN
Aces

CHRIS GOSS ANALYSES AN INFORMAL GATHERING OF BROTHERS-IN-ARMS AND THEIR DESTINIES

No matter what the nationality, countless photographs of airmen in front of their aircraft must have been taken during World War Two. Each one tells a tale.

The quartet of German airmen shown standing in front of a Messerschmitt Bf 109F, taken in August 1941, were from the Stab Schwarm (headquarters flight) of Jagdgeschwader 2 (JG 2) 'Richthofen'. All went on to be awarded the Ritterkreuz and between them, they shot down 353 enemy aircraft. Just one of the four survived the war.

ERICH LEIE
118 VICTORIES

Far left is Oberleutnant Erich Leie, the Geschwader's adjutant. Born in Kiel in 1916, he joined JG 2 in March 1940, shooting down his first aircraft on May 14, 1940. By the end of 1940 he had shot down 11 enemy aircraft and was awarded the Ritterkreuz on August 1, 1941 by which time his tally was 21 'kills'.

In May 1942, he became Gruppen Kommandeur of I/JG 2, but in January 1943 was posted to command I/JG 51 on the Eastern Front. By November 1943, he had shot down 100 aircraft and in December 1944, was given command of JG 77.

Right He was killed on March 7, 1945
'Gulle' Oesau. over Czechoslovakia when his Messerschmitt Bf 109G-14 collided with a Soviet fighter, crashing south of Schwarzwasser. His final score was said to be 118 and he was promoted posthumously to Oberstleutnant.

WALTER OESAU
127 VICTORIES

Second from the left is Major Walter Oesau. Known as 'Gulle', he was born in 1913. He flew with the Legion Condor in Spain, shooting down nine aircraft. At the start of World War Two he commanded 7/JG 51and his first 'kill' came on May 13, 1940.

He was awarded the Ritterkreuz on August 20, 1940 after his 20th 'kill' and then given command of III/JG 51. In November 1940, he moved to lead III/JG 3 and shot down his 40th aircraft on February 5, 1941; the following day he was awarded Oak Leaves to his Ritterkreuz.

He fought in the invasion of the Soviet Union but at the end of July 1941, was recalled to the Western Front to command JG 2, by which time he had been awarded Swords to his Ritterkreuz.

'Gulle' scored his 100th 'kill' on October 26, 1941 but his operational flying was restricted by the Luftwaffe afterwards and he scored just another four victories before being posted to a staff

position in July 1943. Four months later, he was given command of JG 1 and scored his 127th and final 'kill' on May 8, 1944.

He was shot down in combat with a Lockheed P-38 Lightning flown by Lt James 'Pappy' Doyle of 428th Fighter Squadron's 474th Fighter Group. He was killed while trying to crash-land at Etang des Concessions, Beho, Belgium, and is buried in his family's tomb at Meldorf-Dithmarschen near his birthplace of Farnewinkel.

RUDI PFLANZ
52 VICTORIES

Third from the left is the Gruppen Technical Officer, Oberleutnant Rudi Pflanz. Born in 1914 at Ichenheim, he was serving with 3/JG 2 at the start of the war. His first 'kill' was May 30, 1940 and during the Battle of Britain he moved to Stab I /JG 2 then Stab/ JG 2.

By the end of 1940, he had five 'kills' - some records say eight. He had greater success in 1941, resulting in him being awarded the Ritterkreuz on August 1, 1941. By the end of 1941, he had shot down 23 enemy aircraft. In May 1942, he was given command of 11/JG 2

flying the high-altitude Bf 109G-1.

Having shot down his 52nd aircraft at 15:02 hours on July 31, 1942, he was shot down and killed, possibly by Sgt Bill Kelly of 121 Squadron who claimed a Bf 109 near Le Crotoy. It is believed he crashed at Monchaux-les-Quend and he is now buried at Bourdon German Military Cemetery.

GÜNTHER SEEGER
56 VICTORIES

On the right is Feldwebel Günther 'Hupatz' Seeger, Rottenflieger or wingman to the Geschwader Kommodore. Born at Offenbach in 1918, he joined 3/JG 2 in February 1940, shooting down his first enemy aircraft on June 8, 1940.

By the end of 1940 he had shot down four aircraft, but early in 1941 was posted to be an instructor. He returned to Stab/JG 2 in June 1941 and by the end of that year had shot down 19 aircraft by which time he had again returned to being an instructor.

'Hupatz' was back in the fray with 3/JG 2 early the next year but didn't score his 20th 'kill' until August 19, 1942 when he shot down three Spitfires over Dieppe. He was forced down as well, but was soon back

Above
On the left is Lt Egon Mayer, of 7/JG 2 with, Leie, Oesau and Pflanz in August 1941.

Left
'Hupatz' Seeger.

Left centre
Left to right: Leie, Major Helmut Wick (56 'kills') and Pflanz.

in the air, with Stab/JG 2 before moving to 11/JG 2, which then went to Tunisia in November 1942, and was later re-designated 6/JG 53.

Seeger moved to 7/JG 53 in February 1943 and by the end of the year, he had shot down 45 aircraft, but had to return to Germany to recover from malaria. Leutnant Seeger was awarded the Ritterkreuz and promoted to Oberleutnant in March 1944.

In April 1944, he was flying with 4/JG 53 (which he later commanded) and by the end of the year, his score stood at 54, albeit he had been shot down twice. He scored just two victories in 1945 bringing his final score to 56. After the war he joined the West German Air Force; he died on September 6, 2013. ✠

MESSERSCHMITT
Bf 110

Messerschmitt Bf 110C-3 'M8+GP' of ZG 76, August 1940. *PETE WEST © 2014*

ONE-WAY MISSION

The remains of the Hess Messerschmitt in a Glasgow railway yard, May 1941. *KEC*

Farmhand David McLean took the limping German aviator, who called himself Hauptmann Horn, indoors while the Home Guard was called. Flying at times at very low level, the Bf 110 had led Britain's air defences a merry dance during the evening of May 10, 1941. The pilot had climbed and baled out close to his intended destination, Dungavel House, near Strathaven, south of Glasgow. Using good English, he kept repeating that he had to talk directly to the Duke of Hamilton. By the following day, it was clear that 'Hauptmann Horn' was Rudolf Walter Richard Hess, the Third Reich's Deputy Führer.

Hess wanted to initiate peace talks and devised his one-way trip to see the Duke, then an RAF Wing Commander, who the Deputy Führer believed was a powerful politician with anti-war sympathies. Befriending Messerschmitt test pilot and World War One fighter 'ace' Wilhelm Stör, Hess was tutored on a Bf 108 Taifun and then a company-held Bf 110. Bf 110 3869 factory code 'VJ+OQ', variously described as a 'C-1, a 'D-0 or an 'E-1', was specially fitted out for him and made permanently available at Augsburg's Haunstetten airfield.

Deputy Führer Hess was imprisoned and tried for war crimes at Nuremberg. He started a life sentence at Spandau prison in 1947 and died there in 1987.

A team from 63 Maintenance Unit at nearby Carluke came out to salvage the remains of 'VJ+OQ' and the mangled wreckage was placed in store. Eventually the rear fuselage was taken on by the Imperial War Museum, a fascinating relic of one of the war's most bizarre episodes.

Bf 110Cs of 2/ZG 76 over Poland, 1939.

Close support Bf 110Es of SG 1 in France, 1941. KEC

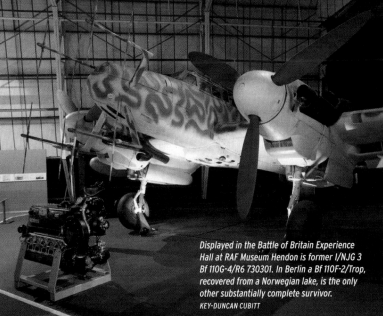

Displayed in the Battle of Britain Experience Hall at RAF Museum Hendon is former I/NJG 3 Bf 110G-4/R6 730301. In Berlin a Bf 110F-2/Trop, recovered from a Norwegian lake, is the only other substantially complete survivor. KEY-DUNCAN CUBITT

MESSERSCHMITT Bf 110G-4

Construction:	A total of 6,170 of all variants were built, including 2,293 'G-4 night-fighter models. The 'G-series was built between December 1942 and April 1945.
First flight:	Rudolf Opitz took the prototype aloft for the first time on May 12, 1936, at Augsburg, Germany.
Powerplant:	Two 1,475hp (1,100kW) Daimler-Benz DB 605B-1 inverted V-12s.
Dimension:	Span 53ft 4in (16.3m) Length, including antennae, 42ft 10in (13.05m) Height 13ft 9in (4.19m) Wing area 414ft² (38.8m²).
Weight:	Empty 11,220lb (5,089kg) Loaded 20,700lb (9,389kg).
Performance:	Max speed 342mph (550km/h) at 22,900ft (6,980m). Service ceiling 26,000ft (7,924m). Range 560 miles (900km) on internal fuel.
Armament:	Two 20mm cannon and four 7.9mm machine-guns in nose, two 7.9mm machine guns in rear cockpit.

Messerschmitt Bf 110G-4/R5 night-fighter.
KEY COLLECTION

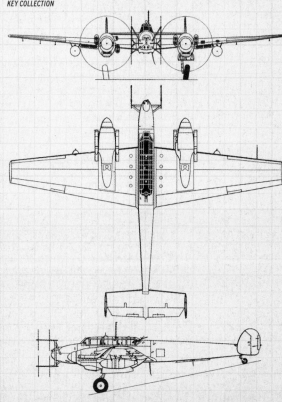

"Manoeuvrability proved surprisingly good for so large a fighter, but the Bf 110 suffered from the same serious fault as the Bf 109 – the automatic slats kept popping out unevenly in tight turns..."

CAPTAIN ERIC 'WINKLE' BROWN - SEE PAGE 97

The Western Desert provided many opportunities for both Allied and Axis forces to inspect each other's hardware: a battle-damaged and stranded Bf 110. KEY COLLECTION

BOMBING *Britain*

HORST ARNSCHEIDT WAS A VETERAN OF 83 'OPS' WHEN A
BEAUFIGHTER CREW MADE SURE THAT HIS 84th WAS ALSO HIS LAST.

CHRIS GOSS RELATES ONE MAN'S WAR

Above
Horst Arnscheidt moved
from the Do 17 with III/KG
2 to the Do 217E.

Three months before his 20th birthday, Horst Arnscheidt began his training as a bomber observer (Beobachter) on January 10, 1940 and took his first flight in a Dornier Do 17 on May 1. From then on, he was associated with the Do 17 and its successor, the Do 217, for the rest of his military flying career. He went on to fly 84 operations, most of them over Great Britain.

His initial training complete, on August 11 he began conversion training on the Dornier 17Z with 10/Kampfgeschwader 2 (10/KG 2) at Achmer in Germany after which he was posted to Oberleutnant (Oblt) Gerhard Schröder's 7/KG 2 based at Cambrai in France.

Oblt Rolf Schweitring was Arnscheidt's pilot on his first operational sortie, which took off at 16:47 hours on September 7th, to attack the London Docks. That date marked the Luftwaffe's first major daylight assault on the British capital. Arnscheidt landed three hours later, noting that there were plenty of fighters and flak over the target.

Horst did not fly with Schweitring again and for some reason he did not take part in the major raids

of September 15; that afternoon Schweitring was killed in a fighter attack, the only casualty in his crew.

Arnscheidt's next flight was with Unteroffizier (Uffz) Rudolf Bodenhagen on the 22nd. For his fourth mission, his pilot was Oblt Rolf Hausner, with whom he then flew for almost two years along with Oberfeldwebels Hartwig Hupe (radio operator) and Ernst Weiderer (flight engineer).

By the end of the Battle of Britain, Arnscheidt had flown 21 operations, all of them against London and all without incident. However, with a shift from mainly daylight to night operations, the start of the Blitz also saw a change in targets. By the end of the year, he had flown 33 missions, again without incident. As well as London, the objectives now included Liverpool (November 28) and Sheffield (December 12) – and, in daylight, an armed reconnaissance (November 7) and an attack on shipping (December 29).

FROM 17 TO 217

After a ten-week break Arnscheidt flew again, returning with his crew to Cambrai in the middle of March

1941, only for them to fly to Vienna at the end of the month. This was in preparation for attacking the Balkans: their first sortie was against Belgrade on April 6.

This part of their war would be short and sharp; just four missions before moving to Athens where they staged another ten over Greece, Crete and the Mediterranean. They were recalled to Germany at the start of June 1941 so III/KG 2 could start handing in its Do 17s for Do 217s.

The Hausner crew had its first experience of the Do 217 on July 10 from Achmer. Training was intense and they did not return to the Western Front until October 28 by which stage III/KG 2 was based at Schiphol, Amsterdam – and even then they did not fly their first mission, an uneventful armed reconnaissance of the English east coast, until January 12, 1942.

LOW-LEVEL CLASH

The crew flew two more sorties in January 1942, attacking Whitby on the 15th and a convoy off Withernsea on the 22nd. On February 12 they deployed to Evreux in France to strike at Exmouth

THE HAUSNER CREW

Rolf Hausner.

What happened to Horst Arnscheidt's original crew of Oberleutnant Rolf Hausner, Oberfeldwebels Hartwig Hupe and Ernst Weiderer? Hausner returned to 7/KG 2 on August 22, 1942, to take over as Staffel Kapitän. Later he was awarded the Honour Goblet.

At 22:15 hours on the night of December 17, 1942, their Do 217 smashed into the hillside at Crow's Nest, Easterside Hill, Hawnby, during an attack on York. The aircraft disintegrated, spilling its bomb load over the hillside. The crew, including Unteroffizier Syrius Erd who had replaced Arnscheidt, were killed instantly. The remains of Hupe and Weiderer were identified, initially buried at Dishforth and now lie at Cannock Chase German Military Cemetery, There was not enough of Erd or Hausner to be buried and, even today, they are still listed as missing.

before returning to Schiphol.

For the remainder of February and all of March, the crew flew six missions, all maritime: mining the Humber on February 27, March 14 and 19, attacking the port of Hull (March 8) and targeting shipping in the Humber (March 13) and a convoy (March 22). Arnscheidt had now flown 57 operations. ➤

Above
A view from the bomb aimer's window of Do 17Zs over England.

Below
A Dornier Do 17Z of KG 2.

out a reconnaissance along the English east coast. An hour later, Bristol Beaufighter I T4917 of 236 Squadron, crewed by Plt Off Laurence Lee and Flt Sgt Taylor, got airborne from Wattisham, Suffolk, to conduct reconnaissance of convoy routes off the Dutch coast.

After a radio failure Lee and Taylor elected to return to base. At 17:12, flying at just 50ft (15m) above the sea to the east of Great Yarmouth, the pair spotted Arnscheidt's Dornier two miles away, flying at the same height. The Beaufighter

gave chase and attacked from the starboard quarter with a two-second burst which went over the Do 217.

The Germans returned fire and Hausner started taking violent evasive action which caught the Beaufighter in its slipstream. The RAF crew managed to get to within 150 yards and opened fire again, apparently hitting the starboard wing root, causing bits to fly off. Hausner deliberately continued to fly erratically but then the Beaufighter's port engine began cutting out and Lee immediately

Above
Bomber observer Horst Arnscheidt.

Right
Rolf Hausner, in peaked cap, in front of 'U5+DR'.

Below
Peter Cleaver and Wallace Nairn in front of their Beaufighter showing his two 'kill' symbols.

After a short break, the four crewmen set off in the early hours of May 9 for Norwich. Arnscheidt noted that the flak was heavy; indeed it accounted for two experienced crews commanded by Oblts Werner Böllert (1/KG 2) and Hermann Obermeier (9/KG 2).

On the 10th, at 15:56, Arnscheidt's Do 217E-4 'U5+BR' lifted off from Schiphol to carry

"At 17:12, flying at just 50ft above the sea to the east of Great Yarmouth, the pair spotted Arnscheidt's Dornier two miles away, flying at the same height. The Beaufighter gave chase and attacked..."

Above
A Do 217E of III/KG 2.

Left
Ofw Ernst Weiderer.

one of which, flown by Feldwebel Franz Koch of 7/KG 2, crashed at Coutances, killing the whole crew. Three more from KG 2 and four from II/KG 40 were damaged.

Arnscheidt flew five times during July. The first sortie was mine-laying on the 12th, with Staffel Kapitän Hauptmann Karl-Heinz Marten as his pilot. Ten days later, Marten was shot down and killed while bombing Bedford and command of 7/KG 2 transferred to a 24-year old Austrian, Oblt Rudolf Graf Thun Hohenstein.

It was back to flying with his usual crew against Birmingham on the 27th, but this was to be Arnscheidt's last time with Hausner, having been assigned as the new Staffel Kapitän's observer. Rolf Hausner and the rest of the crew moved to the headquarters flight, Stab III/KG 2. Arnscheidt next flew a reconnaissance of The Wash and two raids against Birmingham, bringing his total to 80 operations.

In the first three days of August Arnscheidt and his crew attacked a convoy, bombed Norwich and flew a daylight strike against an airfield near Doncaster when they were intercepted by a Spitfire but escaped. Another 7/KG 2 Do 217 ➤

broke off the combat. Undamaged, the Do 217 landed back at Schiphol 17 minutes after the Beaufighter touched down at Wattisham.

MISSIONS INTENSIFY
During the summer of 1942 missions intensified. Hull, Poole, Great Yarmouth and Grimsby were targeted in the remainder of May while the Humber (twice) and Thames estuaries were mined. June saw attacks on Canterbury (twice, as reprisal for Bomber Command attacking Cologne), Ipswich, Poole, Southampton and Weston-Super-

Mare – and mining of the Solent (three times).

All were carried out without incident apart from the trip to Poole on the night of June 3/4. On their return to St Andre in France, the German bombers were followed by two Hurricane intruders of 1 Squadron flown by Sqn Ldr James MacLachlan and Flt Lt Karel Kuttelwascher. Between them, they claimed three Do 217s as destroyed and three damaged at St Andre.

The Hausner crew were forced to divert to Evreux but two Do 217s from KG 2 were shot down,

155

Above
Prisoners of war: Uffz Paulo Bremer is at the back, second left; Horst Arnscheidt is fourth from left.

Right
Fw Franz Koch of 7/KG 2 was shot down and killed by a intruder of 1 Squadron on June 3/4, 1942.

was not so fortunate. Near Kettering, a Spitfire flown by Plt Off Lindsay Black of 485 Squadron RNZAF accounted for Uffz Erich Beyerer and his crew.

CAUGHT BY A PREDATOR

For July and August 1942 the take-off and landing airfield in Arnscheidt's logbook was listed as being Deelen in Holland. On the night of August 7, Do 217 'U5+DR' got airborne from the airfield at 23:00 but was destined to land elsewhere.

Seven crews of KG 2 had received the order to attack an armaments factory in Nottingham. 'U5+DR' was loaded with four 1,100lb (500kg) incendiary containers.

The flight was at low altitude over the North Sea via Texel to the Lincolnshire coast just north of The Wash where the aircraft climbed to 6,500ft. Shortly after crossing the coast, Arnscheidt's Dornier was attacked from the rear.

Plt Off Peter Cleaver and Flt Sgt Wallace Nairn of 68 Squadron had taken off at 22:25 in a Beaufighter from Coltishall in Norfolk on a dusk patrol. At 23:15 they were ordered

Arnscheidt released his pilot's seat belts and then baled out. Oblt Graf Thun then followed.

ASLEEP IN A CORNFIELD

When the speed of his fall had reduced, Arnscheidt opened his parachute and landed in a cornfield, dislocating his ankle. He curled up in his parachute and slept the rest of the night where he had landed. In the morning two frightened young soldiers came and asked:

Left centre
Ofw Hartwig Hupe.

Left
Beaufighter pilot, Peter Cleaver.

"In the morning two frightened young soldiers came and asked: "Where do you come from?" With the answer: "Right from Germany!" Arnscheidt gave up and was taken prisoner."

to return to base but were then given a series of vectors ending in their being put onto an enemy aircraft at 10,000ft.

The Beaufighter chased the enemy for 25 minutes, not helped by it jinking violently 30 to 40 degrees port and starboard and climbing and dropping 1,000ft. Contact was maintained for nine minutes and at last Cleaver managed to get a visual of two exhausts per engine, only for the target to then gradually lose height before levelling off.

Closing to 600ft, Cleaver finally identified the aircraft as a Do 217 and immediately opened fire from behind with a four-second burst. Strikes were seen all over the Dornier and flames appeared from the port engine and fuselage. The

bomber then dived into cloud.

Inside the Dornier, bullets went diagonally through the cockpit but no-one was injured. The left engine burst into flames and the rudders were no longer functioning. Arnscheidt pulled the emergency release for the bombs and the crew quickly began to bale out.

Feldwebel Helmut Kunze, the engineer, was unable to open the emergency hatch in the floor, so Arnscheidt used his torch for Kunze to read the instructions. When the escape hatch was finally opened, Kunze fell straight through the hole, together with the door!

Radio operator Uffz Paulo Bremer had thrown off the canopy roof but he preferred to jump through the opening in the bottom of the cockpit, following Kunze.

"Where do you come from?" With the answer: "Right from Germany!" Arnscheidt gave up and was taken prisoner.

The 68 Squadron crew had seen a big explosion on the ground and three or four fires spread over half-a-mile or more in the vicinity of Coningsby in Lincolnshire. The following day it was confirmed that prisoners had been taken at Revesby Abbey to the east of Coningsby.

Amazingly, all the Dornier's crew members survived. Cleaver visited the crash site of what would be his second and final 'kill' a few days later; little remained of the German bomber. (His first victory had also been a Do 217, on the night of June 24, 1942.)

Following questioning in London, Arnscheidt was taken by train to Scotland but he and another German fighter pilot managed to escape, intending to get to an airfield and steal an aircraft. After three days they were recaptured and he was punished with 28 days' solitary confinement. Horst Arnscheidt, veteran of 84 Dornier operations, did not return to Germany until 1947. ⚡

HEINKEL
He 111

Heinkel He 111H 'A1+ZD' of Stab III/KG 53.
PETE WEST © 2014

HENDON'S **PARATROOPER**

Bench seating, with belts, inside Hendon's He 111H-20/R1. KEY-DUNCAN CUBITT

The Heinkel at the RAF Museum, Hendon, was never a bomber version of the iconic glazed-nosed He 111. Factory code 'NT+SL', 701152 was built from scratch as a 'H-20/R1 transport capable of taking up to 16 paratroopers. What use, if any, it was put to is unknown but by May 1945, Colonel Harold E Watson had it on his 'shopping list' of significant German types for evaluation in the USA – Operation LUSTY. The Heinkel was flown to Cherbourg with the intention of it becoming deck cargo on the carrier HMS *Reaper*, but there were many demands on space, and the He 111 was downgraded in importance.

The story might have ended there, but pilots from the 56th Fighter Group, flying Republic P-47 Thunderbolts from Boxted, Essex, who had been helping Watson gather his treasures, ferried it to their base on July 2, 1945. It was painted with 'stars n bars' national markings and the code letters 'HV-', denoting its allocation to the 56th's 61st Fighter Squadron. The individual code, at times quoted as 'O', was actually a complex overlay of letters, 'O' for Capt J Ordway, 'C' for Major J Carter and 'W' (inner) for Major Williamson; this trio seeming to regard the He 111 as 'theirs'.

The 56th was due to leave for the States in October 1945, so plans were made to 'save' it. It was flown to North Weald on September 12; moving on to Heston on October 14. There it gained RAF roundels and was ferried – its last flight – to Farnborough on November 3 to take part in the extensive German Aircraft Display. It was allocated for museum purposes in 1947 and took up its place at Hendon in May 1978.

A nocturnally camouflaged He 111 of an
unidentified unit, France 1941.

An He 111H of KG 26 carrying a pair of 1,686lb LT F5 torpedoes. *KEY COLLECTION*

The cockpit of Hendon's He 111 with the couch for the gunner/bomb aimer in the extreme nose. Three other substantially intact Heinkel-built examples survive: a He 111E-3 in Spain; a 'P-1 in Norway and an 'H-1 in Germany. About a dozen Merlin-engined CASA 'Pedros' are also extant. *KEY-DUNCAN CUBITT*

HEINKEL He 111H-16

Construction: Around 7,200 He 111s of all variants were built, the majority of which were 'H models. CASA in Spain built 236 He 111Hs under licence as CASA 2.111s, initially with Jumo 211Fs, then with Rolls-Royce Merlin 500s.

First flight: The prototype He 111 V1, D-ALIX, first flew on February 24, 1935. The first of the 'H series flew in January 1938.

Powerplants: Two 1,350hp (1,007kW) Junkers Jumo 211F-2 inverted V12s.

Dimensions: Span 74ft 2in (22.6m) Length 53ft 10in (16.4m) Height 13ft 2in (4.0m) Wing area 943ft^2 (87.6 m^2).

Weights: Empty 19,136lb (8,680kg) Max loaded 30,865lb (14,000kg).

Performance: Max speed 252mph (405km/h) at 19,685ft (6,000m). Service ceiling 21,980ft (6,699m). Range 1,280 miles (2,060km).

Armament: One 20mm cannon in forward fuselage, up to seven 7.9mm machine-guns in ventral, beam and nose positions, plus one 13mm machine-gun in dorsal position. Max bomb load 7,165lb (3,250kg) carried both internally and externally.

Crew: Five - pilot, navigator/bombardier/nose gunner, ventral gunner, dorsal gunner/radio operator, side gunner.

Heinkel He 111H-16. KEY COLLECTION

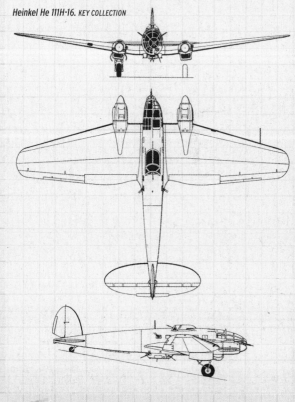

"The Heinkel handled beautifully, being very stable around all axes and offering good harmony of control."

CAPTAIN ERIC 'WINKLE' BROWN - SEE PAGE 97

TURKEY *Shoot*

ONCE A FEARED WEAPON OF WAR, BY 1943 THE STUKA WAS FAST BECOMING A LIABILITY. **ALEKSANDER MEDVED** DESCRIBES THE DAY A SOVIET PILOT SHOT DOWN NINE IN ONE SORTIE

Determined to break the inertia of the advance east designed to crush the Soviet Union, in early July 1943, the Wehrmacht was ready for what was hoped to be a mortal blow. Operation ZITADELLE (Citadel) was launched to encircle the Russians in the Kursk salient. Half way between the Black Sea and Moscow, projecting westwards into what the Germans called the Central Front, the area around Kursk was regarded as a crucial objective.

Soviet high command had acquired detailed breakdowns of the offensive; the forces that would be massed against it and when they would strike. Military planners had achieved superiority both in terms of troops and combat vehicles. Defensive positions had been improved, particularly the ability to engage tanks. Thousands of square miles of hinterland had been mined.

Taking advantage of the sheer scale of the land available to them, the Soviets intended to allow the German forces to roll forward, all the while sapping their strength. When it was apparent that the ZITADELLE advance had been grievously weakened, the Soviet forces would take the initiative, unleashing a tidal wave of men and machinery.

The decision had not been an easy one; two previous summer campaigns had ended in disaster for the Russians, lacking sufficient strength of numbers and suffering from merciless onslaughts from massed tank formations. The latter was still regarded as the main ➤

Below
Ju 87s from StG 2 flew together with StG 77 on the southern flank of the Kursk salient.

> "When it was apparent that the ZITADELLE advance had been grievously weakened, the Soviet forces would take the initiative, unleashing a tidal wave of men and machinery."

"On June 30, 1943 the Luftwaffe had 523 of the cranked-wing dive-bombers on strength, including the newest 'D-5 version, and 442 of these were on the Eastern Front."

Above
Hero of the Soviet Union,
Lt Aleksander Gorovetz.

Above right
Lt Fritz Neumüller of II/
StG 77 celebrating his
500th combat sortie.

Below
Soviet La-5F fighters of
the 302nd IAD on take-off
alert in the early morning
of July 5, 1943.

threat, now that the Wehrmacht was fielding Panther and Tiger tanks, and self-propelled guns. The Luftwaffe also had many Focke-Wulf Fw 190 'Butcher Birds' deployed. It would be a very close-run thing.

IGNORING THE RULES

For ZITADELLE, the Luftwaffe had amassed 2,000 frontline aircraft, about 70% of the German aviation assets on the Eastern Front. Countering this were 2,600 Soviet machines, not including others held in reserve.

To tackle small targets, such as tanks, artillery, command bunkers, etc, the famous Junkers Ju 87 'Stuka' was to be used. On June 30, 1943 the Luftwaffe had 523 of the cranked-wing dive-bombers on strength, including the newest 'D-5 version, and 442 of these were on the Eastern Front.

By spring 1943, German high command had reached some fundamental conclusions concerning the Ju 87. It was still slow and demanded extensive fighter escort.

To achieve satisfactory results, Stukas needed to be employed in very large numbers. Even then, the key to success lay in using part of the force to suppress anti-aircraft fire. Finally, the vulnerable aircraft needed to keep their time over enemy territory to an absolute minimum.

On May 22 that last principle was discarded as Stukas were tasked with striking at Kursk's railway station, a goodly distance behind the lines. Sturzkampfgeschwader 1's II Gruppe (II/StG 1) suffered badly: 36 Stukas took off, nine were brought down by Soviet fighters and nine were badly damaged.

A release by the Sovinformbureau (predecessor of the news agency

Above
*Dive-bombers from II/StG
77 preparing for take-off.*

Novosti) on the 28th, featured the words of captured StG 1 pilot, Lt E Schteimle: "Five kilometres from the target, we were met by the Russian fighters, and the AAA [anti-aircraft artillery] opened with heavy fire. I got rid of the bombs, not reaching the target. ...all our detachment tried to turn to the retreating course.

"But it appeared to be impossible to hold the formation, as Russian fighters were dominant in the air. I saw the aircraft of our detachment going down one after another. A Russian fighter destroyed my engine's radiator, and I was forced to land, too. Here, in captivity, I met the airmen of five crews from my detachment."

HOLDING THE LINE

After the debacle of May 22, the four principles mentioned earlier: large numbers, fighter escort, neutralize enemy flak, minimum time of exposure were re-applied to the Stuka force. Germany's plan for the offensive was to throw massive force at relatively small sections of the front, to overwhelm the ground forces and punch through.

Holding the line, Soviet rifle divisions were slaughtered by a combination of artillery barrage and Luftwaffe ground attacks. The skies overhead were constantly patrolled by large groups of fighters – up to 40 – and when the Stukas arrived the protective shield became even larger.

Although the Red Army Air Force had welcomed a large influx of new aircraft during May and June 1943, this had not been backed up with tried and tested aircrew. The best pilots became commanders at different levels, while the rank-and-file were inexperienced. This was not so for the Luftwaffe, which had not reinforced its units in the East since the spring and its aircrew were well versed in battle.

Up until the Battle of Kursk, it had been very rare for Soviet troops to repulse massive attacks from the Germans. On July 5, the first day of the battle the Luftwaffe staged 1,718 Stuka combat sorties: StG 1 undertaking 518, StG 2 – 487, III/StG 3 – 129 and StG 77 – 584. StG 1 was included within Luftflotte 6 (6th Air Fleet), while Stg 2 and StG 77 were part of Luftflotte 4.

The dive-bombers of the 1st Air Division, Luftflotte 6, were assigned the northern portion of the Kursk salient and were attacking the Soviet 13th Army. Luftflotte 4 was to destroy the defensive positions of the 6th Guards Army, to pave the way for the tanks of the 2nd SS Corps.

FLAGGING MORALE

From the beginning, the Luftwaffe inflicted a heavy toll on the enemy, exploiting the raw nature of many of the Soviet pilots. The records of the Soviet 286th Fighter Division well illustrate this. During July, only four of the 59 Lavochkin La-5s brought down were piloted by seasoned veterans. That 59 was more than half of the combat effectiveness of the three regiments making up the division.

Such losses impacted upon the morale not only of the 'rookies', but also the veterans. For several days the Luftwaffe basked in air superiority.

Soviet leaders understood only too well how fast their divisions and regiments were fading away. Transfers from the forces held in reserve to the danger zone began far earlier than anticipated. But these reserves were even more lacking in combat skills; the ability to repel the enemy was being diluted by the day. Air force high command believed that a morale boost was vital to help turn the tables and fortunately one was soon found.

Reports for the 8th Fighter Division (Istrebitel'naya Aviatsionnaya Diviziya - IAD) dated July 6 described a sortie by the 88th Guards Fighter Regiment (Istrebitel'niy Aviatsionniy Polk ➤

LOSS OF THE KNIGHTS

Knight's Cross Ju 87 pilots killed during the Battle of Kursk

Name	Unit	Date	Sorties
Kurt-Albert Pape	3/StG 1	July 7	350
Karl Fitzner	5/StG 77	July 8	550
Bernhard Wutka	8/StG 2	July 8	500
Günther Schmid	5/StG 2	July 14	700
Egbert Jaekel	2/StG 2	July 17	983
Walter Kraup	III/StG 2	July 17	310
Friedrich Lorenz	1/StG 1	July 17	350
Willi Hörner	7/StG 2	July 21	500

Right
Soviet La-5 pilots posing for a publicity shot.

Below
Photo-journalist of the Red Army's frontline newspaper, Natalya Bode, posing on a crashed Ju 87.

- IAP) between 19:50 and 20:20 hours. Fifteen La-5s were covering troops in the Vladimirovka-Kochetovka district in the southern sector and the 88th IAP was engaged in a dogfight with six Ju 88, escorted by five Bf 109s. Two of the bombers were downed and one was damaged.

Deputy leader Lt Aleksander K Gorovetz failed to return. For some time it was unclear what part he had played in the La-5 versus Ju 88 and Bf 109 fight but it eventually became clear that he had been involved in an air war all of his own and one that had inflicted the heaviest toll on the Luftwaffe.

ONE AGAINST NINE

Three days later, the 8th IAD's headquarters received a message from the front explaining that a solo La-5 had wreaked havoc among Ju 87s on July 6. Those watching the spectacle included the 242nd tank brigade commander, Lt Col A F Smirnov and – from his command post – General Nikolai Fyodorovich Vatutin.

Documents of the 8th IAD, dated July 9 stated: "...a new group of nine Ju 87s appeared. Guards Lt Gorovetz immediately broke into the enemy bomber formation. As the result of the first attack, two Ju 87s were destroyed and two more collided in mid-air trying to evade our fighter's attack.

"The rest of the Ju 87s broke formation and circled, preparing to bomb our land troops. Continuously attacking from the vertical manoeuvre, Lt Gorovetz brought down the rest – five bombers. But in turn he was himself attacked by the group of Me 109s. [They] set his plane on fire and began chasing it, until it crashed 6km to the south of Oboyan. Our land troops were amazed by Lt Gorovetz's dogfight and reported to the division command post ...about the heroic deed of the unknown fighter pilot."

It seems that a radio malfunction prevented Gorovetz from informing his group leader of his sighting of the Ju 87s, which explains why he went into the attack alone. Gorovetz's wingman, Lt V M Rekunov lost his leader during the initial dogfight and had no idea of his comrade's fate. (Rekunov perished in an air combat on August 12.)

The lone La-5's antics were seen in the distance by Lt B Artyukhin of the 88th IAP. He was engaged in combat with Messerschmitts and couldn't come to Gorovetz's assistance. Despite all the military witnesses and civilians in nearby villages, the exact number of enemy aircraft brought down by Gorovetz still cannot be confirmed.

When General Vatutin discovered that the man he had seen fighting so courageously despite being outnumbered had died as a result of the action, he did two things. He told members of the 242nd Tank Brigade to search for the wrecks of Gorovetz's victims. He also initiated the award of Hero of the Soviet Union. When the men came back

Above
A German rescue team inspecting the wreckage of a Ju 87.

Left
Soviet soldiers inspecting the remains of a Stuka.

"...the battles of Kursk took a terrible toll of the Ju 87 force. Leading Stuka 'ace' Hans-Ulrich Rudel witnessed the carnage: 'Bitterness and bereavements nearly smashed us.'"

in from their search they reported nine Stuka wrecks, but they could give no confirmation of precisely *when* these had fallen.

SLAUGHTER OF THE KNIGHTS
According to Luftwaffe data, on July 6 five Ju 87s crashed in territory occupied by Soviet troops, one more force-landed just after crossing the front line upon return and four were damaged. The Germans consider that only three of these losses were caused by fighters, the rest were due to ground fire. The records make no note of a mid-air collision.

The fog of war may have contributed to this but it must not detract from the sacrifice of Aleksander Gorovetz, who crashed very close to his home airfield. Most probably he was brought down by Messerschmitts of 7/JG52, which claimed the destruction of a lone La-5 at 20.20, Moscow time.

It cannot be denied that losses of some Red Army Air Force units on July 6 were even higher, but the battles of Kursk took a terrible toll of the Ju 87 force. Leading Stuka 'ace' Hans-Ulrich Rudel witnessed the carnage: "Bitterness and bereavements nearly smashed us." During the 17 days of combat

at the Kursk salient, the Luftwaffe lost eight dive-bombing 'aces', each one had been awarded the Knight's Cross.

FINDING A HERO
When Gorovetz's La-5 crashed it did so almost vertically and at high speed, ploughing deep into the ground. In the hope of identifying the pilot, members of a tank unit tried to pull the wreck out of its crater by attaching a tow rope around the La-5's wooden tail section. The result was predictable – the rear fuselage detached from behind the cockpit.

There was one other witness to Gorovetz's famous sortie. As a young boy, S Sergeyev also saw the impact. In 1957, after serving in the Soviet Navy, he decided to locate the exact spot.

He found it, near the village of Zorinskiye Dvory. Excavations revealed the pilot's remains and thanks to fragments of documents that had survived within the pocket of his mouldering tunic, Alexander Gorovetz was identified.

A report from the 2nd Air Army's political directorate, summed up the last moments of a Hero of the Soviet Union. "He alone, in the unequal combat with enemy aircraft, brought down nine Ju 87s. Comrade Gorovetz himself, in this fight being mortally wounded, died as a hero, not managing to fly four kilometres to his airfield. The Soviet warrior's air battle was observed with amazement by ground troops, who confirmed its results."

With many thanks to Gennady Sloutskiy for his help in this feature. ✠

JUNKERS
Ju 87

Glykol
50/50

L1

SNOWBIRD

The name 'Stuka' comes from the German for dive-bomber: Sturzkampflugzeug. Stukageschwader 5 (StG 5) was formed in Norway in January 1942 and, flying a mixture of Ju 87Ds and 'Rs, served in Finland and on the northern elements of the Eastern Front against the USSR. Ju 87D 'L1+CB' carries hastily-applied snow camouflage for operations in the Kola Peninsula, around Murmansk. This machine featured extended wings and additional windscreen armour – no siren was fitted to the undercarriage. For rearward defence it had two MG 81 7.9mm machine-guns.

PETE WEST © 2014

There are only three substantial Stuka survivors; an 'R-2 in Chicago, another 'R-2 in Berlin that was salvaged from the Murmansk area and the RAF Museum Hendon's 'G-2 494083. Hendon's is thought to have been built as a Ju 87D-5 and modified as a 'G-2 with the capability to mount 37mm cannon under the wing. It is not known what, if any, operational flying it did. It has called Hendon its home since 1978.
KEY-DUNCAN CUBITT

JUNKERS Ju 87B-1

Construction:	About 5,700 of all models were built.
First Flight:	The prototype, Ju 87 V1, first flew at Dessau in the spring of 1935. It was powered by a Rolls-Royce Kestrel V and featured twin fins and rudders. The V2 flew in the autumn of 1935 with single fin and a Junkers Jumo 210A.
Powerplant:	One 1,200hp (895kW) Junkers Jumo 211Da 12-cylinder piston engine.
Dimensions:	Span 45ft 3in (13.79m) Length 36ft 5in (11.09m) Height 13ft 2in (4.01m) Wing area 343ft² (31.86m²).
Weights:	Empty 5,980lb (2,712kg) Max loaded 9,560lb (4,336kg).
Performance:	Max speed 211mph (339km/h) at sea level. Service ceiling 26,250ft (8,001m) Range 370 miles (595km).
Armament:	Two 7.9mm machine-guns in the wings, one 7.9mm machine-gun in the rear cockpit. One 1,102lb (499kg) bomb under the centreline.

"Once settled down to the cruise the feeling of vulnerability became almost oppressive, probably accentuated by the high position of the pilot's seat and the good visibility through the large glasshouse canopy."

CAPTAIN ERIC 'WINKLE' BROWN - SEE PAGE 97

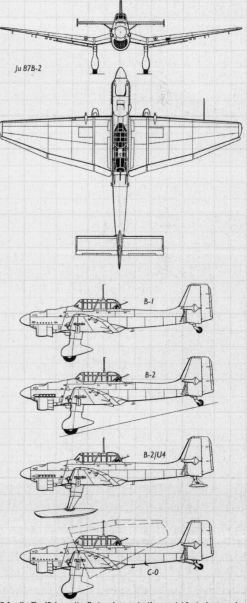

Ju 87B-2

B-1

B-2

B-2/U4

C-0

Ju 87B family. The 'B-1 was the first major production model featuring a major redesign of the fuselage, undercarriage and tail and the 'B-2 had further refinements. A field modification, the Ju 87B-2/U4 featured skis. A small number of navalised Ju 87C-0s were built in 1939, with an arrester hook and manually-foldable wings, intended for the aircraft carrier 'Graf Zeppelin', which was not completed. KEY COLLECTION

Stukas of StG 1 over the English Channel during the summer of 1940.

FELLING *Giants*

THE LUFTWAFFE'S LONG-RANGING FW 200 CONDORS WERE VULNERABLE AS THEY RETURNED TO THEIR BASES. **CHRIS GOSS** DESCRIBES HOW ALLIED INTRUDERS CULLED THE MIGHTY WARRIORS

Always associated with the Battle of the Atlantic, the massive four-engined Focke-Wulf Fw 200 Condor first made its presence known over Norway in 1940. In the years that followed it saw some success in the bomber and reconnaissance roles but, as the war progressed it became increasingly vulnerable.

With fewer than 300 built, serviceability and the availability of spares plagued the Condor's effectiveness. Long-ranging Allied fighters, acting as intruders – intercepting Luftwaffe aircraft close to their own bases as they returned from a sortie – found Fw 200s relatively easy prey.

The first of a Condor probably July 31, 1942. Mosquito, Wg Hoare recorded loss to an intruder occurred on Flying a DH Cdr Bertie and Plt Off Sydney Cornes of 23 Squadron claimed an unidentified aircraft at Orleans. That day an Fw 200C-3 of IV Gruppe/Kampfgeschwader 40 (IV/KG 40), flown by Oberleutnant Hermann Frenzel on a training flight, crash-landed and burnt out. - Frenzel and one other crew member were wounded.

It was 1944 before a Condor was again downed by an intruder. Flt Lt Charles Scherf and Fg Off Al Brown in a 418 Squadron RCAF Mosquito shot down a Condor ➤

Below
Loading a 550lb bomb onto a Condor of I/KG 40.

Above
The Fobker crew – Kipp and Fobker are on the far left.

Right
The waist gun position on a Condor; it was through this that Artur Steig managed to escape.

Below
Condors were prone to structural failure or engineering problems – 'F8+FW' of 12/KG 40 suffered a broken back.

of 9/KG 40 near Avord, France, on January 27. Oberfeldwebel Willi Schmidt and four crew died. Two days later, four Hawker Typhoons of 247 Squadron, led by Wg Cdr Erik Haabjoern, caught an example from 12/KG 40 south of Chateaudun. Feldwebel (Fw) Karl Miklas and three of his crew and passengers were killed.

STUMBLING ON SHIP-KILLERS

Obergefreiter Artur Steig was a ground engineer. In October 1943, he was sent to Peenemünde on Germany's Baltic coast for training on glider-bombs. He joined III/KG 40 at Avord on February 4, 1944. The day after he arrived, Steig was told that the unit would be attacking a convoy in the Mediterranean but that they had to fly to Cognac in western France.

There, the Condors were to be loaded with the Henschel Hs 293 radio-controlled bombs. The winged missile was designed to glide towards its target, then a rocket motor would ignite for the final plunge.

Steig's Fw 200C-4, flown by Haupt Ingeniur Anton Leder, took off as planned but had to turn back because of weather. As they were taxiing out, Avord came under attack from USAAF Boeing B-17 Fortresses. Artur recalled: "...to prevent our Condors

from being destroyed, we were ordered to take-off immediately. That meant aircraft took off in all directions and, to avoid a collision, our plane had to turn and begin a new take-off run. We had luck as we were not hit by bombs but now our plane was completely alone in the sky..."

A total of 547 B-17s were raiding five different airfields and they were shadowed by 210 'Little Friends', a mixture of Lockheed P-38 Lightnings, Republic P-47 Thunderbolts and North American P-51 Mustangs.

One of the escorting units was the 20th Fighter Group (FG) flying P-38s from Kings Cliffe. They took off from their Northamptonshire base at 09:12 hours, rendezvoused with two combat

wings of B-17s south of Le Havre and escorted the bombers to their target at Orleans. As they approached Avord the American pilots spotted 12 "large aircraft" preparing to take-off.

After four were airborne, Colonel Barton Russell, the Group Commander, ordered the 77th Fighter Squadron (FS), commanded by Lt Col Robert Montgomery, to attack, leaving the 55th FS to give top cover and the 79th to remain with the bombers.

This was not strictly an intruder mission, as the fighters had other instructions. But it was a classic case of capitalising on a 'target of opportunity', made possible by the increased endurance of escort fighters by 1944.

Lt Jack Davies was acting as wingman to *White Leader*, Captain Paul Sabo. Jack: "We spotted a Fw 200 flying down on the deck at about 1,000ft altitude and headed south. We attacked at once, descending in a 270 degree right turn down to 500ft, and from the left-hand side. The left waist gunner was clearly visible and firing at us as we approached.

"Sabo and I, firing simultaneously, must have hit the Fw 200's fuel tanks or some other explosive

"Sabo and I, firing simultaneously, must have hit the Fw 200's fuel tanks or some other explosive material, resulting in a major explosion. We went up and over the Fw 200 in a climbing turn and saw [it] crash on fire into the ground. I said to myself if anyone escaped that crash it would be a miracle..."

material, resulting in a major explosion. We went up and over the Fw 200 in a climbing turn and saw [it] crash on fire into the ground. I said to myself if anyone escaped that crash it would be a miracle..."

FULL FUEL - FLYING BOMB

Artur Steig said: "Our Fw 200 had been refuelled with 6,000 litres before and, because of the attack, the fuel tanks burst into flames. Our pilot and one of the gunners were killed instantly and because we mechanics had not been given parachutes, the 2nd Pilot, Unteroffizier Kurt Frosch, announced that he had decided to try an emergency landing.

"I think it was more of a crash than an emergency landing, and when I regained consciousness, the whole plane was on fire, as were my clothes. The plane's fuselage had rolled over several times so the machine-gun mountings had been ripped out, which made it

possible for me to climb out. Two of my comrades were then killed by exploding ammunition after they had left the plane..."

The crash occurred at St Juest, 6 miles (10km) south-west of Avord. Four crew were killed and three injured, with one of the ground crew killed and two, including Steig, injured. Burns to Artur's hands were so serious that he was in hospital, initially at St Dieux and then Orleans, until the end of June 1944.

GEAR DOWN, BIG TARGET

Intruder attacks continued to result in losses of Condors and casualties among both air and ground crew. For example, on March 5, 1944, Mustangs of the 4th FG and 357th FG accounted for a number of Condors during a low-level attack on Cognac.

A luckier crew came from Stab III/ KG 40 and almost fell victim to two

Mosquitos from 151 Squadron on the evening of June 22. Ironically, their call-signs were *Snoozy 34* and *Snoozy 41*. Flt Lt Len Gregory DFC's combat report related: "We sighted a large aircraft about three to four miles range, dead ahead on a southerly course. We were closing range rapidly when [it] turned onto an easterly course, at the same time lowering its undercarriage. It then became evident that the aircraft intended to land at Cognac, so we increased speed.

"By the time range had closed sufficiently for an attack to be carried out the aircraft, which was identified as an Fw 200, [it] was well on the approach run. *Snoozy 34* [Fg Offs B C Gray and L T Gorvon) gave a three-second burst. Strikes seen on port mid-fuselage.

"*Snoozy 41* gave a two to three second burst from 1,500 yards

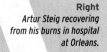

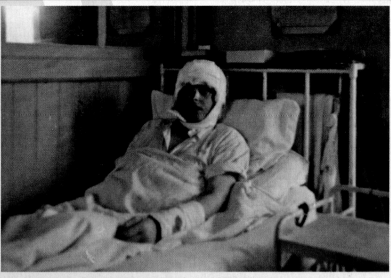

range. E/a [enemy aircraft] height below 50ft; four to five strikes seen on port outer engine. E/a continued to touch down and run along the runway quite normally. Fairly intense flak had opened up on us and we carried on to next objective..."

Damage to the Condor was slight but it did result in the death of Flieger Ingenieur Anton Wagner.

DOWN BUT VULNERABLE

By now, the skies over Europe were a dangerous place for a large and lumbering aircraft like the Fw 200. Through a mix of unserviceable aircraft, lack of spares and losses in action, Condors were becoming rare beasts.

Feldwebel (Fw) Otto Kipp was an experienced radio operator with III/KG 40. His operational flying had started with 8/KG 40 Heinkel He 111s in the summer of 1941. Shortly afterwards he and his crew, commanded by Leutnant (Lt) Herbert Fobker, were shot down by two Spitfires of 266 Squadron; the four of them spending 116 hours in a dinghy.

The crew converted to the Fw 200 and were quite successful, until Fobker's luck ran out on the last day of 1943. His brother explained: "Herbert had to abort a mission early due to engine problems, so he returned to Cognac. Just after he landed; the airfield was attacked by American bombers, and he and his crew had to hurry into slit trenches. As fate would have it, the trench he chose received a direct hit and he was killed..."

Otto then flew with Fw Heinz Grauber but, on July 5, 1944, they fell victim to an intruder. "We were

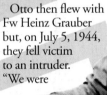

ordered to fly to an auxiliary airfield located at the so-called Charentes-meadows. This was so the aircraft would be protected from the daily fighter-bomber attacks.

"We took off early in the morning; we had been told there were no enemy aircraft in our airspace. However, this proved to be wrong and we were attacked by a Lightning just after take off, at an altitude of 160ft. Our plane burst into flames and so we had to make an emergency landing in a cornfield, where farmers were harvesting..."

INEVITABLE RESULT

The Condor's attacker was Captain Art Jeffrey of the Wattisham-based 434th FS, 479th FG. Thirteen P-38 Lightnings of the 434th arrived over Cognac just after 09:00 and immediately spotted the Condor taking off.

Jeffrey's combat report outlines the inevitability of the

"The pilot then made a belly-landing, and by the time the ship had stopped skidding the whole plane was ablaze."

situation: "My right wingman called over the radio that a plane was taking off. Since my Flight was closest, I called *Newcross Leader* to furnish top cover while I went down for a pass.

"The plane had made a 180 degree turn to port and was staying on the deck, close to the airdrome and town. There was quite a lot of flak being shot at us from this area.

"I came at the e/a from the front, making a 180=degree overhead pass and setting up for a stern shot at him. I began firing at about 350 yards, closing to about 50 giving him about a ten-second burst. The right inboard engine caught fire immediately and parts flew off it. The pilot then made a belly-landing, and by the time the ship had stopped skidding; the whole plane was ablaze. I observed one man making his escape from the front of the ship..."

Amazingly, half of the crew emerged from the rear of the burning Condor without injury and the three that were, including Otto Kipp, were only lightly wounded. Sadly, the mechanic Unteroffzier Otto Kiphut was killed by a single bullet to the head.

The last Condor had been killed by an Allied intruder. From then on, Condors were used entirely in the transport role. The last one confirmed as being lost in action was an Fw 200D-2 on September 27, 1944, operated by Lufthansa. It was shot down near Dijon by Captain Harold Augspurger and 2nd Lt A G Petry in a Beaufighter of the USAAF's 415th Night Fighter Squadron. For the remaining months of the war, Condors were all but extinct. ✠

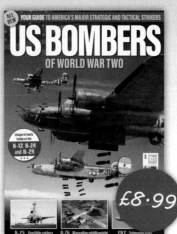
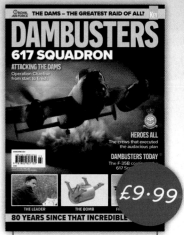

FOCKE-WULF *Fw 200*

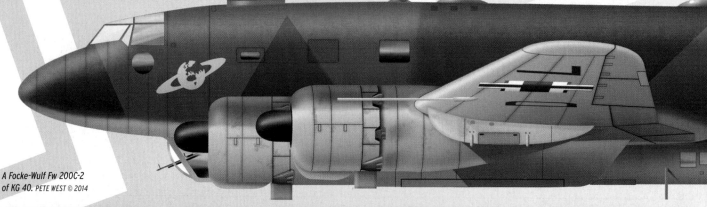

*A Focke-Wulf Fw 200C-2
of KG 40. PETE WEST © 2014*

AIRLINER TURNED **WARRIOR**

Flying the Lufthansa flag, Fw 200A D-AMHC 'Nordmark' in 1938. This machine was taken over by the Luftwaffe as a transport, call-sign 'F8+MV'; it was lost in the USSR in 1943. LUFTHANSA

When the Dornier Do 17 and the Heinkel He 111 first appeared, Germany was at pains to emphasise that these designs were airliners or mailplanes. As Focke-Wulf's talented designer Kurt Tank set about designing the Focke-Wulf Condor it was intended only to be an airliner, with no thought to military applications. When the company was asked to create a long-range anti-shipping bomber from the Fw 200, it lost no time; the first militarised example, the Fw 200 V10, appearing in 1939.

National airline Lufthansa was the launch customer, followed by Danish Air Lines and the appropriately-named Sydicato Condor in Brazil. Lufthansa continued to operate Condors during the war on flights to neutral countries; its last service ended in disaster in April 1945 when an Fw 200B-2 was lost on a flight from Berlin to Barcelona.

'F8+DB' of Stab I/KG 40.

Fw 200s of I/KG 40 at Bordeaux, 1941.

FOCKE-WULF Fw 200C-3

Construction:	280 of the airliner and military versions were built, the last eight coming off the production line in 1944.
First Flight:	Airliner Fw 200 V1 D-AERE first flew on July 27, 1937, powered by four Pratt & Whitney Hornets. The military Fw 200C-0 first appeared in September 1939.
Powerplant:	Four 1,200hp (895kW) BMW-Bramo 323 R-2 Fafnir 9-cylinder radials.
Dimensions:	Span 107ft 9^1/$_2$in (32.85m) Length 76ft 11^1/$_2$in (23.45m) Height 20ft 8in (6.29m) Wing area 1,290ft^2 (119.8m^2)
Weights:	Empty 28,550lb (12,950kg) Max loaded 50,045lb (22,700kg)
Performance:	Max speed 224mph (360km/h) at 15,750ft (4,800m) Service ceiling 19,000ft (5,791m) Range 2,760 miles (4,441km)
Armament:	One 7.99mm machine-gun in forward dorsal turret, one 13mm machine gun in aft dorsal position, two 13mm machine guns in the beam hatches, one 20mm cannon in forward ventral position and a 7.9mm in aft ventral position. Up to 4,626lb (2,098kg) of bombs.
Crew:	Seven or eight

Focke-Wulf Fw 200C-8/U10 with Henschel Hs 293 rocket-powered glide-bombs. KEY COLLECTION

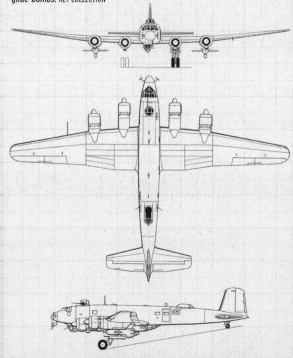

"...in concert with the U-boat, the Condor so nearly brought Britain to her knees in 1940-1941. But as a fighting machine the Condor possessed all the shortcomings that were to be expected of a converted commercial airliner..."

CAPTAIN ERIC 'WINKLE' BROWN - SEE PAGE 97

Fw 200C 'F8+AB' of Stab I/KG 40, September 1941.

CHERISHED
Mementoes

ARTUR BUCHERT WAS AWARDED A 'POKAL' OR GOBLET FOR
HIS PART IN LONG-RANGE SORTIES. **CHRIS GOSS** INVESTIGATED HIS STORY

Above
A Ju 88T of 2/123.

Right
*A dramatic photo taken by
the Weixelbaum crew of
Spitzbergen, Norway.*

Treasured by collectors for their fine detail on solid silver or nickel silver and above all for the special achievement they honour, 'Pokal' goblets are also very scarce. One that does survive is a lasting tribute to Oberfeldwebel Artur Buchert.

Reichsmarschall Hermann Göring established a new award, the Ehrenpokal der Luftwaffe, on February 27, 1940. Translating as 'Honour Goblet', its name was shortened by many to Pokal, it was presented only to flying personnel. By December 1944 in the region of 58,000 had been issued 'on paper' although around 13 to 15,000 goblets were actually awarded.

Born in Mulkenthin in Pomerania on March 28, 1914, it is not known precisely when Buchert joined the Luftwaffe, but he was recorded as

"It is thought that the Weixelbaum crew flew about 152 operations against Britain..."

being a member of 2 Kompanie Luftnachtrichten Abteilung 6 (an Air Signals unit) at Königsberg-Balliet in September 1939. In April 1941 he was a radio operator flying with 1 Staffel (Fern)/Auflklärungsgruppe 120 (1st Squadron of Long Range Reconnaissance Wing 120 or 1(F)/120) based at Stavanger-Sola in Norway.

VETERAN OVER BRITAIN

Commanded by Major Andreas Schub, 1/120 had been in action from the start of the war over Poland, Norway and by the spring of 1941, Britain. Buchert crewed up with 23-year old pilot Leutnant Helmut Weixelbaum and observer Feldwebel Dietrich Beyer.

The Weixelbaum crew was first mentioned in Luftwaffe records on June 5, when they dropped bombs on an industrial target in the north of Scotland. British records report a target near Aberdeen being hit.

Next mention is an attack on a railway yard near Newcastle on November 22, then damaging to a ship off the British coast on December 3, followed by damage to two ships between Scotland and the Faroes on January 6, 1942.

By this time, the regular crew comprised: recently-promoted Oberleutnant Weixelbaum (pilot), Leutnant Dietrich Beyer (observer), Artur Buchert (radio operator) and Unteroffizier Arno Schäfer (flight engineer). All of them had been awarded the Eiserne Kreuz ('Iron Cross' – EK) first and second class so the next award would not be long in coming.

The Pokal could be awarded to aircrew who had achieved first ➤

Above
The Weixelbaum crew, after return from a mission in 1941. Left to right: Schäfer, Beyer, Weixelbaum, Buchert.

Left
Artur Buchert's Ehrenpokal.

or second class EKs, but whose performance was not yet considered to merit the Deutsches Kreuz in Gold (German Cross in Gold) or the Ritterkreuz (Knight's Cross).

Weixelbaum was presented with his Pokal on February 6, 1942, Buchert and Beyer received theirs on May 25, 1942. It seems that Arno Schäfer had to wait until June 1943 for his. It is interesting to note that Buchert's Pokal is inscribed May *18*, 1942, perhaps the opportunity for the presentation being delayed. Their pilot, Weixelbaum, went on to be awarded the Deutsches Kreuz on September 8, 1942 – the only member of the crew to receive it.

It is thought that the Weixelbaum crew flew about 152 operations against Britain before the crew appears to have been posted. For Buchert and his pilot, this meant joining 2/123 at Athens-Tatoi. Weixelbaum was promoted and given command of the Staffel in January 1944.

Ich verleihe
dem

Feldwebel
Karl Ludwig
in Anerkennung seiner hervorragenden Tapferkeit
und der besonderen Erfolge als Aufklärungsflieger

den Ehrenpokal
für besondere Leistung
im Luftkrieg

Hauptquartier des Ob. d. L., den 31. August 1943

Der Reichsminister der Luftfahrt
und Oberbefehlshaber der Luftwaffe

Göring

Reichsmarschall

DEUTSCHES ROTES KREUZ · SUCHDIENST

Aufn. LND	**Heimkehrer-Erklärung**	Benachr. LND

Bildlisten-Band LH Seite 5d mit / ohne Bild

TEIL A
Personalien des Kriegsversch.: (lt. Bildliste) des Heimkehrers: VA angelegt.

Die Erklärung wird abgegeben:

1) über den Kriegsverschollenen Buchert Arthur 28.3.14
   Name   Vorname   Geb Datum
   Feldp.-Nr. / off. Einheit / Lager: Aufklärungs Staffel 2 (F) 123

2) von dem Heimkehrer: Hagmann Heinrich
   Name   Vorname
   Remagen /Rhein Deichweg 3
   Vollständige Jetzt-Anschrift

3) für die Angehörigen
   der Angehörigen:

TEIL B

TAZ a) Den Kriegsverschollenen habe ich selbst als Toten gesehen am ... Er ist gefallen/verstorben während des Einsatzes: ... / in Gefangenschaft: ...

TD b) Ich hörte, daß der Kriegsverschollene am ... gefallen/verstorben sei während des Einsatzes: ... / in Gefangenschaft: ...

LAZ c) Den Kriegsverschollenen habe ich selbst am ... in Gefangenschaft gesehen im Lager Nr. ... Ort ...

LD d) Ich hörte, daß der Kriegsverschollene am ... in Gefangenschaft geriet. Lager Nr. ... Ort ...

HK e) Der Kriegsverschollene ist am ... aus Gefangenschaft entlassen worden. Ich habe ihn nach seiner Heimkehr zuletzt gesehen am ... in ...

LvAZ f) den Kriegsverschollenen habe ich selbst am ... schwer verwundet gesehen. Ort: ... Art d. Verwundung: ...

LvD g) Ich hörte, daß der Kriegsverschollene am ... schwer verwundet wurde. Ort: ... Art d. Verwundung: ...

NHW h) Der Kriegsverschollene befand sich noch am August 1944 bei obiger Einheit / im obigen Lager. Bei Einheitenangabe Einsatzort: Alexandrien

NHW i) Der Kriegsverschollene wurde am ... versetzt zu / verlegt nach Einheit / Lager: ... Ort: ...

NHW k) Über den Verbleib des Kriegsverschollenen kann evtl. nähere Auskunft geben:

Isny, den 17. Febr. 1962

MEDITERRANEAN ENCOUNTER

Little is known about their time in Greece, until the night of September 4, 1944. Weixelbaum together with Buchert, Leutnant Horst Wolfarth and war correspondent Karl Ottahal lifted off in Junkers Ju 88T-3 330231 '4U+KK' to carry out a photo-reconnaissance of Alexandria, Egypt.

Horst Wolfarth recalled: "That night we had orders to photograph the harbour of Alexandria. Take-off took place at dusk, and we climbed to an altitude of 9,000m. As the outline of the port began to emerge in the light of the moon, we went a little lower. Then the wireless operator shouted: 'A night-fighter!' and immediately he began to shoot. I turned around, but saw no pursuer.

"Meanwhile, the night was lit up by tracer bullets. We went into a dive, but the plane was seriously damaged. The radio operator threw off the cabin roof... I was taken out of the plane by the stream of air. I knew that I had to free-fall for some time, because we had been flying very high, in an oxygen-poor zone. At first I could not find the handle of the ripcord but when I finally pulled it, it was like being struck by a giant's fist."

In a letter to Frau Weixelbaum in March 1946, Wolfarth added more: "Our plane was attacked north of Alexandria by night-fighters. We had a short air combat. A little later, when we went into a dive to escape from the fighter planes flying behind us, I got a terrible blow and I was thrown out of the machine. The cause of this event, I do not know.

"Then, still at night, when I was swimming in the sea I saw that not very far away from me distress flares were fired. I firmly believed that I was swimming near my comrades. How great was my disappointment when at the dawn of the day none of my comrades could be seen, only the sea... This was about 80km north of Alexandria.

"When I had been discovered by a British aircraft, and later rescued, I reported the observation of these distress signals and asked to send a plane to search for my comrades. Whether this wish was granted, I do not know. Eight days later, an English officer told me the bitter news that up to this point none of my comrades had been found. Here in the prison camp, I have investigated further, but not seen, nor heard of them…"

No Allied night-fighter claims were filed that night so who or what caused the demise of this Ju 88 is not known. Sadly, the bodies of Weixelbaum, Ottahal and Buchert were never found and all three are still listed as missing in action. ✠

Clockwise from far left
Artur Buchert, sporting his awards. From the top: Frontflugspange für Aufklärer (reconnaissance clasp), Luftwaffe Long Service ribbon, Eiserne Kreuz first class and the radio operator's badge. In the middle he wears the EK second-class ribbon.

The award document for the Pokal. This one belongs to another recce pilot who was reported missing in Russia in 1943.

Official confirmation from the German Red Cross, dated 1962, declaring Artur Buchert as missing, believed dead.

Lapel badge worn by members of 2/123.

TIP-AND-RUN *Raider*

CHRIS GOSS EXPLAINS WHY USING THE OTHERWISE SUPERB Fw 190
AS A NOCTURNAL FIGHTER-BOMBER WAS A DISMAL FAILURE

Below
Fw Richard Wittmann of 2/SKG 10 with a tank-equipped Fw 190.

By February 1943, the Luftwaffe's bomber arm was suffering heavy losses. Dornier Do 217s and Junkers Ju 88s were due to be replaced by the Ju 88S, Ju 188 and Heinkel He 177. These new types were believed to be better equipped to attack Britain and defend themselves against RAF night-fighters. But they were behind schedule for service entry.

It is believed that the initiative of using Focke-Wulf Fw 190s by night against targets in south-east England – and as a means of harassing London – came from the recently-appointed Inspekteur der Kampfflieger and Angriffsführer England, Oberst Dietrich Peltz. Success of daylight 'tip-and-run' tactics by Fw 190s indicated the type could be an ideal interim night bomber. It was believed that the effectiveness of daylight fighter-bomber attacks was diminishing rapidly because of the increased efficiency of British defences; this assumption was flawed.

The suitability of the Fw 190 for its new role was to be brutally proven wrong on the very first mission.

FULL MOON, NO CLOUDS
The first attack was planned for April 16, 1943, because it was a cloudless night with no haze and a full moon.

The raid was mainly carried out by II Gruppe/Schnellkampfgeschwader 10 (2nd Wing of Fast Bomber Group 10 – II/SKG 10) which had been flying daylight missions from the start of March 1943.

They were in trouble well before the English coast. Oberleutnant (Oblt) Franz Schwaiger of 2/SKG 10 was killed when his aircraft developed technical problems and crashed near Abbeville. Experienced Oblt Rudolf Trenn, Staffel Kapitän of 3/SKG 10, collided with two other Fw 190s on take-off from Poix in northern France. Trenn was killed, the other two pilots were uninjured and three '190s were written off.

Having been briefed earlier that day, II/SKG 10 flew to Amiens-Glissy where they were armed with either a 551lb or 1,102lb (250kg or 500kg) bomb and two 66-gallon (300-litre) underwing drop tanks. Oblt Werner Dedekind, Staffel Kapitän of 7/SKG 10, led some eight aircraft of his Staffel from Amiens at about 23:30 hours, flying in pairs to and from the target. A single '190 from II/SKG 10 was damaged during a take-off accident.

A similar number of Fw 190s followed from Hauptmann (Hptm) Hans-Curt Graf Von Sponeck's 5

Staffel. It is believed some members of Oblt Josef Keller's 6 Staffel also took part.

The raid was a total disaster, with no perceptible damage caused for the loss of ten Fw 190s, three of which landed at West Malling in Kent. Four pilots were killed and three were taken prisoner.

POOR PREPARATION
Oblt Kurt Dahlmann, a replacement for one of the night's losses, later cited a number of reasons why the inaugural mission was a failure. Some pilots from II/SKG 10 had only flown daylight sorties while others had no combat experience at all. Within I/SKG 10, only former Stuka pilot Hptm Edmund Kraus, 1 Staffel Kapitän, had any combat blind flying time, albeit limited, and none had been over the UK. The remainder, even if they had operational experience, were *exclusively* daylight ground-attack pilots.

Raids were to take place only during the full moon period – or in the six days before or after – and in no more than three-tenths cloud. Navigational aids, light beacons, high-power radio beacons and a ground direction-finding station ▶

Above
Loading an Fw 190 with an SC 500 bomb.

Left
Oblt Rudolf Trenn was killed in an accident taking off from Poix. He was posthumously awarded the Ritterkreuz.

operations were dismal failures. Based at Manston, the Typhoon-equipped 609 Squadron noted in its diary for May 17: "It is without many tears that the squadron today learns that it will no longer be required to man searchlight boxes – the thing is considered a flop, partly owing to inadequate squitter control on Typhoon Identification Friend or Foe sets."

The reason for such a sudden change in RAF anti-Fw 190 tactics was the success the night before of 85 Squadron's Mosquitos. The unit's diarist related: "After an hour or so, it was clearly seen that the Typhoons were unable to cope so the 11 Group Controller risked his bowler hat and grounded them, thus enabling the 85 Squadron Mosquitos to go in and deal with the '190s which they did in no uncertain manner."

Above
Oblt Kurt Dahlmann (second from left, as a Major in 1944) listening to Generalfeldmarschall Hugo Sperrle. On the right are, left to right: Oblt Walter Starck (1/SKG 10), Oblt Erich Richter (2/SKG 10) and Oblt Rudolf Wagner (3/SKG 10).

Right
Aircrew of 85 Squadron, many of whom had success against I/SKG 10 for the remainder of 1943.

were considered key to success.

A comprehensive system of light beacons had been established along the French coast from Dunkirk to Abbeville, backed up by three lines of radio beacons sited on the coast, 12 miles (20km) inland and 24 miles inland – but these aids assumed the pilots were experienced in night flying.

Dahlmann later wrote: "The large number of light beacons only served to bewilder the pilots. Owing to the pilot's general state of agitation and the cramped conditions in the cockpit of the Fw 190, the pilot found that by the time he had ascertained the location of the light beacon and worked out the course to the nearest airfield, he was already many kilometres away from the light beacon as his last known fixed position and was heading in the wrong direction."

The raid of April 16, 1943 was a victim of poor preparation, the absence of control and the inability of pilots to navigate a single-seater at night in a combat zone. In particular, searchlights and flak proved disconcerting and the exploding anti-aircraft shells were far more unnerving in the dark. More worryingly, the night 'Jabos' had yet to encounter any RAF opposition.

A small number of II/SKG 10 aircraft are said to have tried other attacks on London during the nights of April 18 and 20. About this time, I Gruppe began to concentrate on nocturnal missions and II Gruppe reverted largely to daylight ones, before moving to the Mediterranean in June.

To improve effectiveness, night bombing techniques and navigation training intensified, but even this had its hazards, especially when RAF intruders interfered.

Briefed to carry out a nuisance attack on London, about 18 Fw 190s operated over areas of Kent, Essex, Hertfordshire, Buckinghamshire, Surrey and Sussex on the night of May 16/17, dropping bombs in several places and inflicting some damage and casualties.

TYPHOON OR MOSQUITO?

The RAF meanwhile was concerned at its lack of success against fast night fighter-bombers. According to the 85 Squadron diarist, until that night it was thought the de Havilland Mosquito was unable to catch an Fw 190 but single-seat Hawker Typhoons would be able to intercept while patrolling 'boxes' created by the searchlight units.

This notion was based on the Typhoons' ability to combat daylight tip-and-runs, but anti-night 'Jabo'

GOING TO WORK

He continued: "Sqn Ldr Green and Flt Sgt Grimstone were first to go to work. Under the control of Sandwich, they patrolled the Channel for some time at 10,000ft and then having got a vector of 040 degrees increased height to 18,000ft.

"Pilot got a contact and closing rapidly got a visual at 1,000ft range of an Fw 190 with long range tanks and a bomb under the fuselage. Pilot opened fire with a short burst from dead astern at 100 yards range whereupon the e/a [enemy aircraft] blew up with a large red flash, the Mosquito having to dive sharply to port to avoid the burning debris… They have the honour of being the first night-fighters to shoot down an Fw 190 over this country at night."

The night did not end there, the diary continuing: "Flt Lt Howitt and Fg Off Irving were the next… Following the searchlights, they got a contact dead ahead at 8,000ft over the sea near Hastings. Losing height down to 4,000ft, pilot got a visual of a Fw 190 which had been taking evasive action.

"Pilot got in a long burst from dead astern at 600ft. Strikes and a vivid flash were observed and pieces of burning debris flew off the e/a which fell away to port. Pilot followed down and gave the e/a another long burst whereupon it caught fire and dived into the sea.

"Fg Off Thwaites and Fg Off Clemo took off at 00:05 hours. Controlled by Sandwich, they chased an enemy aircraft across the sea but were called off when approaching the French coast. Pilot then got a contact below, crossing from starboard to port... Obtaining a visual of an Fw 190, pilot closed to 50 yards range and opened fire whereupon the e/a blew up and went down in flames... Some of the debris was seen in the air intake on landing.

"Pilot, having been given a vector of 350 degrees, obtained another visual of an Fw 190 and opened fire at 200 yards range. A vivid flash was seen. The e/a lost height and pilot following it down gave it three more bursts and vivid flashes were seen. E/a now appeared to be going down and a large object was seen to come away from the top of it. Pilot then overshot and was unable to see if the e/a crashed, and therefore this Fw 190 was claimed as probably destroyed. **>**

"After an hour or so, it was clearly seen that the Typhoons were unable to cope so the 11 Group Controller risked his bowler hat and grounded them, thus enabling the 85 Squadron Mosquitos to go in and deal with the '190s which they did in no uncertain manner."

Above
Heinz Ehrhardt (left) as a guest of 609 Squadron.

Below
An Fw 190 of I SKG 10 at dispersal.

range. E/a exploded with a huge orange flash and went down in flames crashing near Gravesend."

This Fw 190 could be seen plummeting out of the sky from 85 Squadron's dispersal at West Malling.

All of this chronicled another disastrous night for Hptm Helmut Brücker's I/SKG 10. The claims however were slightly optimistic. John Shaw's 'kill' can be positively matched to Unteroffizier (Uffz) Wilhelm Schicke of Stab (headquarters flight) I/SKG 10 who crashed at Higham,

Gravesend, at 02:05. The only other loss that night was Leutnant Walter Strack of 3/SKG 10 who simply 'failed to return'. Four Fw 190s from I/SKG 10 landed at either Dieppe or Poix with varying degrees of combat damage, but with no injuries to their pilots.

WALKING IN

Undeterred, I/SKG 10 attacked London the following night with nine aircraft. Results were again indifferent with one Jabo of I/SKG 10 landing at Fécamp with 25% combat damage. Fg Off John Lintott of 85 Squadron claimed a '190, seeing it crash and burst into flames in the Thames Estuary. It was flown by the experienced Oblt Paul Antwerpen whose body was washed ashore in Belgium almost four months later.

The Fw 190s of I/SKG 10 returned to the fray on May 19/20. For one German pilot it was a repeat performance of the first night. No.609 Squadron's Operational Record Book relates: "At about 03:30, the hard-pressed Duty Intelligence Officer suffers his final nervous breakdown when into the Intelligence Office there walks, amongst other pilots, a pilot of the Luftwaffe.

"Shortly afterwards, 609's IO is roused by Flt Lt Wells bounding into his room and shouting 'Heard the news? We've captured a '190!'

"Fg Off Shaw and Fg Off Lowton took off at 01:25. A contact was obtained at two miles range slightly below and to port. The Mosquito was then caught in the searchlights which held it for about five minutes in spite of continuous flashing of the letter of the period, and prevented pilot from obtaining a visual.

"Contact, however, was maintained and eventually a beam of the searchlight illuminated the target which pilot identified as an Fw 190 with long range tanks and bomb under the fuselage. Pilot closed in underneath and opened fire at about 100 yards

"Obtaining a visual of an Fw 190, pilot closed to 50 yards range and opened fire whereupon it blew up and went down in flames... Some of the debris was seen in the air intake on landing."

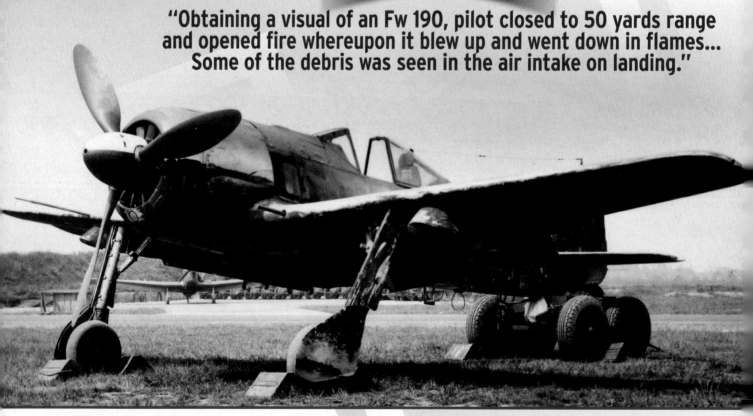

"This again was apparently wrong and I am fairly convinced I was being intentionally misled by the enemy. I was off course, off time and had lost navigation completely. This together with my lack of experience at night missions (I had been trained as a Stuka pilot) convinced me I was over some French air base when the airfield lighting was turned on and I landed… at Manston."

A DROP IN THE OCEAN

Two nights later, about eight Jabos carried out nuisance attacks on London, Ashford and Dover, losing Uffz Fritz Kolz of 3/SKG 10 who was shot down by Sqn Ldr Edward Crew of 85 Squadron. From May 20 there was a flurry of massed daylight tip-and-run attacks by II, IV and occasionally I/SKG 10 before these inexplicably ceased completely on June 6 – and II and IV Gruppen were moved to the Mediterranean.

From June, I/SKG 10 became a 'jack of all trades' until the autumn. Bombing missions by night over

Left
Preparing an Fw 190 of I/SKG 10 for a mission, 1944.

"It appears that the pilot, lost, has been beckoned to Manston by searchlights and landed. Seeing this, the CO, Wells, Van Lierde and Renier have dashed out to the aircraft by car where Sqn Ldr Ingle, making up in volume what he lacked in lingo, pointed his finger and shouted repeatedly 'Hands Up! Hands Up!' which the German (incidentally covered by the guns of a Beaverette armoured car) obliged by doing…"

Uffz Heinz Ehrhardt of 2/SKG 10 recalls that losses were so bad on April 16/17 that I/SKG 10 was withdrawn and moved to Cognac in south-west France. There, pilots practised night flying, returning to Amiens about a month later. Ehrhardt's first mission was against London on May 17/18 when he

successfully dropped his bomb on what he thought were the docks.

His next sortie was on the eventful night of May 19/20. "Approaching London, we could request a bearing from a station on the continent. After pushing a button, we received a three-digit number giving the heading following by a two-digit number representing the minutes to fly the course.

"When I requested my first bearing, the information was obviously wrong, heading me out to sea. I therefore turned 270 degrees, carrying me to the outer flak barrier at London. After being picked up by a searchlight, I was handed over to the next and so forth until I released my bomb, dived to increase speed and requested another bearing.

England, daylight fighter sorties over the Reich, night operations over France, daylight sorties over France against returning bombers, reconnaissance and weather reconnaissance sorties over England – all of these were expected of the Gruppe. When the Allies invaded mainland Europe in June 1944, I/SKG 10's priorities changed yet again, earning it the nickname of the 'Fire Brigade'.

Kurt Dahlmann of I/SKG 10 summed up the Fw 190 nocturnal raids against London as: "not very successful. It was really makeshift. This type of aircraft was neither designated for this kind of mission nor was it suitable for this task." He added that the whole episode was: "little more than a drop in the ocean". ✠

Above
Hiding an Fw 190 of I/SKG 10, Normandy, June 1944.

FOCKE-WULF
Fw 190

A Focke-Wulf Fw 190F-8 'Schlachtflugzeug' close-support fighter with an ETC bomb rack under the centre section, carrying a 551-pounder, plus four underwing 110lb bombs. PETE WEST © 2014

SECOND AND THIRD GENERATION

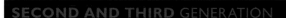

Focke-Wulf Fw 190D-9 'White 12' of II/JG301. PETE WEST © 2014

From the very beginning Kurt Tank's Fw 190 showed exceptional promise and that it was capable of evolving. In 1944 the advent of the 1,776hp (1,324kW) liquid-cooled Junkers Jumo 213A-1 offered the chance to drop the bulky radial and smooth out the 'Butcher Bird'. In May 1944 the Fw 190 V17/U1 served as the prototype for the Fw 190D series. Widely known as the 'Dora', the type was longer that its predecessors. The first production examples, 'D-9s, entered service with JG 54 in late 1944.

With the next iteration of the Fw 190 family, the Reichsluftfahrtministerium (RLM - German Air Ministry) honoured Kurt Tank by using the prefix 'Ta' for his designs. With long-span wings and a Jumo 213E, the Fw 190 V18 served as the prototype for what became the Ta 152H. High-flying, the series included a pressurised cockpit, going operational with JG 301 in early 1945. Those pilots who flew the 'Dora' quickly realised what an exceptional fighter it was, and the Ta 152 series promised great things. As with other German designs, for both it was a case of too few, too late.

The fifth Ta 152H-0, 0005, on the compass-swinging circle at Cottbus, early 1945. KEC

Fw 190s of I/SG 5 at Pori, Finland, 1944.

The RAF Museum has two Fw 190s, 'A-8/R6 733682 at Cosford and two-seater Fw 190F-8/U1 at Hendon (illustrated). About 24 Fw 190s survive as substantial airframes, including an Fw 190D-9 at Wright-Patterson and a Ta 152H with the National Air and Space Museum, both in the USA. The Musée de l'Air at Le Bourget has a French-built NC.900. As well as the originals, Flug Werk produced new-build FW 190s – several are airworthy.
KEY-DUNCAN CUBITT

The cockpit of a captured Fw 190A.
KEY COLLECTION

FOCKE-WULF Fw 190A-8

Construction:	20,051 Fw 190s of all models were built, including 4,677 Fw 190As, by Focke-Wulf, Ago, Fieseler and Arado and in France as the NC.900. From the mid-1990s Flug Werk built a series of new-build versions, designated FW 190, several of which are flying.
First Flight:	The Fw 190A V1 prototype first flew on June 1, 1939, carrying the civil registration D-OPZE, in the hands of Focke-Wulf chief test pilot Hans Sander.
Powerplant:	One 1,700hp (1,268kW) BMW 801D-2 14-cylinder radial.
Dimensions:	Span 34ft 6in (10.5m) Length 29ft 0in (8.83m) Height 13ft 0in (3.96m) Wing area 197ft^2 (18.3m^2).
Weights:	Empty 7,000lb (3,175kg) Loaded 10,802lb (4,899kg).
Performance:	Max speed 408mph (657km/h) at 20,600ft (6,280m). Service ceiling 37,400ft (11,399m). Normal range 500 miles (804km).
Armament:	Two 13mm machine-guns in nose and four 20mm cannon in wings. One 1,100lb (500kg) bomb under centre section. Bombs, rockets, torpedoes and other stores on some models.

Focke-Wulf Fw 190A-3.
KEY COLLECTION

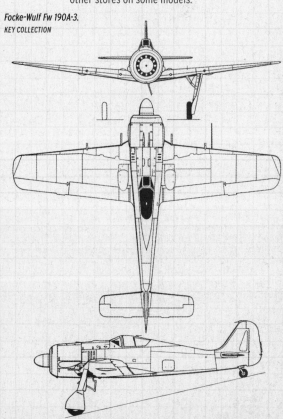

"A superb fighter with outstanding rate of roll. The 'Dora' or 'D-9 version is German fighter technology at its best."

CAPTAIN ERIC 'WINKLE' BROWN - SEE PAGE 97

HORNET'S *Sting*

CHRIS GOSS HIGHLIGHTS INTRUDER MISSIONS BY THE LITTLE-KNOWN ME 410, AN ADVANCED AIRCRAFT RARELY USED TO ITS FULL POTENTIAL

Below
Me 210s on trial in Tunisia, 1942.

Following the failure of the Messerschmitt Me 210 as a credible replacement for the Messerschmitt Bf 110, the Luftwaffe pushed ahead with the Me 410 Hornisse (Hornet), which first appeared at the end of 1942. It was essentially the same as the Me 210 but fitted with Daimler Benz 603 engines.

The initial version was the Me 410A-1, designed as a light bomber with fixed forward-firing machine-guns and cannon, two rearward firing remotely-controlled cannon and an internal load of two 2,200lb (1,000kg) bombs.

Hornets first appeared over Britain in the summer of 1943. Luftwaffe chiefs had decided that II Gruppe of Kampfgeschwader 40 (II/KG 40), which had been attacking British targets with Dornier Do 217s, would operate the Me 410A-1 as V/KG 2, commanded by German Cross in Gold holder Hauptmann (Hptm) Friedrich-Wilhelm Methner.

Flying at night, aircraft would bomb airfields and other targets as well as attacking RAF bombers taking off or returning from missions over Europe if the opportunity arose. The logbook of Unteroffizier (Uffz) Albert Wolk, a radio operator with 4/KG 40, shows he started converting at Memmingen together with his pilot, Uffz Heinz Holzmann, on June 5, 1943 before moving to Lille-Vendeville from where they flew their first operation in a Me 410 of 14/KG 2, an intruder mission in the Cambridge area, in the early hours of August 23.

BOMBER AND INTRUDER

The first intruder 'kill' by a Hornet was on the night of August 23 by Feldwebel (Fw) Heinz Graeber, radio operator/gunner to Knights Cross holder Oberleutnant (Oblt) Wilhelm Schmitter of 15/KG 2. Of the seven crew on board Lancaster III EE105 of 97 Squadron, returning from a raid on Berlin, only one was killed.

The unit's first losses in action were Fw Franz Zwissler and Oberfeldwebel (Ofw) Leo Raida on the night of July 13, victims of Flt Lt Nigel Bunting's 85 Squadron de Havilland Mosquito off Felixstowe. The next was Hptm Friedrich-Wilhelm Methner two nights later, probably a victim of Flt Lt Bernard Thwaites of 85 Squadron off Dunkirk. Methner was replaced by Major Wolf-Dieter Meister as Gruppen Kommandeur.

Operations and successes were sporadic and, as the year progressed, fewer intruder missions and more bombing sorties against London became the norm. This appears to coincide with the appointment of Oberst Dietrich Peltz as the commanding officer of IX Fliegerkorps in August 1943 after which he attempted to co-ordinate attacks on England. Apparently Peltz thought the Hornet was better suited as a bomber than an intruder.

The logbook of Oblt Rudolf Abrahamcik of 14/KG 2 provides a good example of what V/KG 2 was then doing.

operations in an aircraft that proved itself inferior to American day fighters. (Abrahamcik noted another three Tagjagds in November as well as four attacks on London.)

TARGETING LONDON
British defences, both flak and fighter, were becoming far more potent, as proven by losses – six in September, five in October and, in November, five more, including Hptm Wilhelm Schmitter, Staffel Kapitän of 15/KG 2, and Albert's Wolk's former pilot, Heinz Holzmann, on the night of the 8th.

December 1943 was much quieter with V/KG 2 concentrating on ➤

Left
Detail view of the 13mm MG 131 rearward-firing barbette on a Me 410.

Below
Working on an Me 410's Daimler Benz 603.

Bottom
Images of Me 410s in service are rare: a KG 2 'A-1.

It reports his first mission – an intruder – following conversion from the Do 217 as August 18. (This was his 134th of the war, the previous 133 being with I/KG 2 and 6/KG 40.) There were further intruder flights on September 4, 7, 24 and 28, the last resulting in him shooting down Lancaster III JA965 of 101 Squadron, killing all eight on board. This was the final recorded intruder victory by V/KG 2 for 1943.

In October Abrahamcik flew just one mission, which unusually was a Tagjagd, or daylight fighter sortie, on the 18th. Such sorties show how misguided the Luftwaffe was by employing experienced night bomber aircrew on daytime

"Flying at night, aircraft would bomb airfields and other targets as well as attacking RAF bombers taking off or returning from missions over Europe if the opportunity arose."

Right
Oblt Rudolf Abrahamczik.

Below
An Me 410A-1 of KG 2.

London. Abrahamczik reported missions on the 1st, 10th, 20th and early morning and late night on the 21st. The only loss during this time was Leutnant (Lt) Heinz-Günther Baack of 14/KG 2 on the 19th.

The combat report of Plt Off Doug Robinson and Fg Off Terry Clark DFM of the Bristol Beaufighter-equipped 488 Squadron RNZAF relates what happened: "A contact was obtained at 12 o'clock, range two miles, with the e/a [enemy aircraft] well above so pilot climbed to 25,000ft and obtained a visual on an Me 410, 2,000ft ahead and slightly below... pilot closed to 250 yards and opened fire with a two to three-second burst but owing to vapour trails no strikes were seen.

"The e/a took violent evasive action, climbing and diving in tight turns, but the searchlights illuminated and held the e/a and our pilot plainly saw the black crosses on the wings.

"A second attack was made from 150 yards, closing to 100, several short bursts during which strikes were seen on the port engine and fuselage, a red glow appearing from the engine. Inaccurate tracer from the barbettes was passing above our aircraft and the pilot made his third attack from 100 yards with a two-

"A contact was obtained at 12 o'clock, range two miles, with the enemy aircraft well above so pilot climbed to 25,000ft and obtained a visual on an Me 410, 2,000ft ahead and slightly below..."

second burst, and pieces flew off the e/a which did a steep port turn and dived towards the ground. The visual was temporarily lost but the aircraft was seen to hit the ground and explode shortly afterwards..."

BABY BLITZ
The New Year saw little change in V/KG 2's modus operandi. Ofw Hermann Bolten had joined 13/KG 2 on August 29, 1943, having been part of the Erprobungsstaffel Me 210 at Lechfeld since the end of May 1942, operationally testing the new Me 201. He then moved to Erprobungsstaffel Me 410 to do the same for the Hornet.

With 14/KG 2, he flew two intruder missions in September 1943 and two intruder, three bombing and two Tagjagd flights in October. He was credited with the shooting down of a four-engined bomber on October 18.

In January 1944 Bolten flew seven attacks against London, an increase commensurate with the start of Operation STEINBOCK or, as it was known by the Allies, the 'Baby Blitz', which began on the 21st.

That first night, Knights Cross holder Hptn Kurt Heintz, the Gruppen Kommandeur of V/KG 2 for just over three months, was lost.

Bolten also had time to fly a Tagjagd on January 11, when he and a number of other pilots were credited with shooting down a four-engined bomber. STEINBOCK continued into February with another six missions for Bolten.

The last was a nuisance raid on London in the early hours of the 22nd, when he was attacked and badly damaged by a night-fighter. This was probably Flt Sgt Tom Bryan and Sgt Basil Friis of 96 Squadron in a Mosquito, who claimed an Me 410 destroyed. Bolten reported being hit in the port engine and crash-landed at Abbeville at 03:17 hours, which matches well with the RAF crew's combat report:
"I attacked from 150 yards with two short bursts. Target was then dead ahead and slightly above, now flying a fairly steady course, height 17,000ft. There were strikes in the port engine, the e/a took violent evasive action and returned my fire

though his aim was wide. I followed him and fired another short burst with no results. E/a now throttled back violently and did a vertical bank to port. I overshot below him and noticed no exhaust flares were visible on the port engine...
I lost my visual as he dived steeply away..."

RETURN TO INTRUDING
Although more missions were flown against London on February 22, 24 and 29 and again on March 2, V/KG 2's part in the Baby Blitz was changing. The unit was redesignated II/KG 51; its crews, including Gruppen Kommandeur Hptn Karl-Egon von Dalwigk zu Lichtenfels, and the aircraft moving as well. It would appear that the 'U5' fuselage codes denoting KG 2 were retained until at least March 22 when they were replaced by KG 51's '9K'. At the end of the month II/KG 51 recommenced intruder operations.

At the same time, I/KG 51, commanded by Hptn Hans Unrau, arrived at St Andre in France and began pure bombing missions. **>**

Above
Hptm Karl-Egon von Dalwigk zu Lichtenfels.

Above
Two Ritterkreuz winners from 6/KG 51: Fw Hanns Trenke and Ofw Hans Frach, late 1944.

Germany but not before Oblt Georg Csurusky was credited with shooting down two Halifaxes on the night of May 7-8.

MIXED FORTUNES

For II/KG 51, this period of success was about to improve – temporarily. Radio operator Fw Gustav Delp of 6/KG 51 thought he had shot down a P-47 Thunderbolt at dawn on April 21 but it was a Miles Master of Peterborough-based 7 (Pilot) Advanced Flying Unit.

The next night Hornets of II/KG 51 followed B-24 Liberators back to their bases after a daylight raid on Hamm in Germany. Ten "Halifaxes and B-17s" were claimed between 22:05 and 22:26 when actually *nine* B-24s of the USAAF's 389th, 448th, 453rd, 458th and 467th Bomb Groups were lost. It was not one-sided and two Me 410s were lost to return fire: Oblt Klaus Krüger and Fw Michael Reichardt of 6/KG 51 were both killed when their Hornet crashed at Ashby St Mary in Norfolk while the Hornet flown by Hptn Dietrich Puttfarken and Ofw Willi Lux simply disappeared.

Despite these losses, a second wave of intruders set forth later that night with Uffz Walter Brügel of 4/KG 51 shooting down an Armstrong Whitworth Albemarle of 42

Its first combat losses were Lt Horst Eppendorf and Uffz Günter Zaprodsky of 2/KG 51 who were killed crash-landing near Beauvais returning from a sortie on March 15.

The first recorded 'kill' of this new intruding phase was made by Major Meister, now Geschwader Kommodore of KG 51, on March 30-31, the night of RAF Bomber Command's disastrous Nuremberg attack. Twelve days later, Lt Wolfgang Wenning accounted for an American B-17 Flying Fortress of the 96th Bomb Group while Knights Cross holder Hptn Dietrich Puttfarken, Staffel Kapitän of 5/KG 51, probably shot down a Stirling of 1654 Conversion Unit and, unusually, a Spitfire of 64 Squadron.

The same two pilots claimed a Halifax of 625 Squadron and a Lancaster of 115 Squadron respectively on the night of April 18/19. Oblt Klaus Bieber of 5/KG 51 also shot down another Lancaster of 115 Squadron that night.

All this was being achieved without loss – which is more that can be said for I/KG 51, which had up to April 22 lost nine aircraft and 16 aircrew killed or missing. The following month it was pulled back to

RARE SURVIVORS

Cosford's Me 410 in a rare moment out in the open. KEC

The RAF Museum's Hornisse is well known, but another has spent most of its time in reclusive store in Maryland in the US, awaiting display by the National Air and Space Museum (NASM). The American example, Me 410A-1/U2 10018, was the first to be captured, at Trapini, Sicily, in August 1943. It was shipped to the US for trials and had arrived at Wright Field, Dayton, Ohio, by October 1944. By 1946 it had been handed on for museum use, transferring to the NASM.

Part of the 'Warplanes' display at Cosford, Shropshire, Me 410A-1/U2 420430 was captured at Vaerlose, Denmark, and ferried to the Royal Aircraft Establishment at Farnborough, Hampshire, arriving there on October 13, 1945. It was moved into storage in December and joined the RAF Museum's collection at St Athan, Wales, in 1960.

Me 410A-1/U2 10018 at Wright Field, USA, circa 1945. KEC

> "The enemy aircraft was obviously unaware of the Mosquito's presence and as the range was opened to about 70 yards slightly below and astern, the tail light of the Me 410 blotted out the spot on the ring sight."

Operational Training Unit.

The remainder of April saw four more victories, albeit one was Pyrrhic. Lt Wolfgang Wenning, II/KG 51's technical officer, collided with his victim, an Oxford of 18 (Pilot) Advanced Flying Unit, killing himself, Fw Gustav Delp and Plt Off Moore.

With the build-up to the invasion of Normandy, more RAF intruders were making their presence felt over occupied Europe. Oblt Klaus Bieber and his radio operator were killed near Beauvais on May 12, possibly by Flt Lt Harry White and Fg Off Mike Allen in a 141 Squadron Mosquito. They were the first of a number of victims of RAF intruders over the next two months.

May 29 proved to be a bad night for II/KG 51 when a pair of Me 410s collided on take-off from Gilze-Rijen, Netherlands, with one crew killed the other injured. A 6/KG 51 Hornet was shot down off Cromer while engaged in an intruder sortie in the Cambridge area by Wg Cdr Mike Wight-Boycott and Flt Lt Douglas Reid of 25 Squadron; Fw Ernst Dietrich and Uffz Walter Schaknies were reported missing.

ON THE DEFENSIVE

June 1944 saw a shift in emphasis following the invasion of Normandy but II/KG 51 suffered heavily at the hands of intruders, night-fighters and flak either over England or the beachhead. Two Hornets were lost to intruders while engaged on Nachtjagd sorties, three to anti-aircraft fire, and one to fighters over the beaches.

The last 'kills' over England occurred on June 28 – a Lancaster of 90 Squadron fell to Lt Anselm Markau, a B-24 of the 801st Bomb Group to Uffz Franz Wachtler of 4/KG 51 and an unidentified Stirling to Lt Friedrich of 5/KG 51. From now on, all but one of the losses (which included Markau and Wachtler) occurred over France – to the extent that, within a month, II/KG 51 ceased operations on the Me 410. It was withdrawn to Germany for conversion to the Me 262 jet.

Uffzs Walter Brügel and Rudolf Sperlich of 4/KG 51 had been tasked to carry out an intruder sortie over East Anglia on the night of July 25 and were apparently headed for home when they were spotted by a Mosquito of 515 Squadron, itself returning from an intruder mission of the Böblingen/Stuttgart area. Whether in error or as an aid to recognition by the German flak, the Me 410 was burning navigation and tail lights, which made it easy for former 'Dambuster' Sqn Ldr 'Micky' Martin DSO DFC and Fg Off John Smith who pounced just off the coast at Knokke in Belgium.

The RAF crew's combat report records: "The enemy aircraft was obviously unaware of the Mosquito's presence and as the range was opened to about 70 yards slightly below and astern, the tail light of the Me 410 blotted out the spot on the ring sight. This inconvenience was adjusted with no trouble at all and the ring sight moved to the 'Hun's' starboard engine; a short burst of cannon set the engine well alight.

"This obviously shook the 'Hun' and he speedily dived to port but an almost instantaneous short second burst of cannon fire directed at the port wing blew the wing off and the enemy aircraft, burning well, went down in a screaming dive and was seen to crash on the sea and continued burning." The last Me 410 intruder sortie over the UK had come to a tragic conclusion. ✂

Above
Mosquitos of 96 Squadron.

LEVIATHAN *Killers*

IN 1943 THE LUFTWAFFE BEGAN USING A NEW WEAPON WITH
DEVASTATING RESULTS, AS **TOM SPENCER** RECOUNTS

n the clear skies of a Mediterranean September afternoon, above an iridescent azure sea, a formation of twin-engined aircraft neared its target. Ahead were the foaming white wakes of an impressive fleet of 19 warships steaming at speed.

Within minutes, the attackers had left the largest of them sinking, ripped apart by a massive explosion that took more than 1,200 men to their deaths. The vessel was the flagship of the post-Mussolini Regia Marina (the Italian Navy) the 42,000-ton battleship *Roma*. It had become the most significant victim of the PD-1400X or 'Fritz X' radio-

guided bomb. The era of precision-guided munitions, so common on today's battlefields, had arrived.

The Fritz X was based on the PC 1400 3,000lb (1,360kg) ballistic bomb designed to penetrate armour and concrete with a warhead containing 705lb of Amatol explosive. The weapon was fitted with a cruciform wing and a segmented annular tail with electromagnetically-activated spoilers that gave control in pitch and yaw. By remotely 'flying' the Fritz, it could provide unparalleled accuracy, essential against moving targets such as ships or against small fixed targets like bridges.

An FuG-203 Kehl III/FuG-230b Strassburg guidance package was fitted which received inputs from the bomb aimer who steered it via a control panel joystick. The weapon was tracked through the standard Lofte 7 bombsight, aided by a smokeless white/blue flare or lamp mounted in its tail.

Live testing on the Fritz X was conducted at Peenemünde during the early months of 1942 with drops from a Heinkel He 111 producing encouraging results. For operational use He 177s and Dornier Do 217s were the designated launch platforms. (For more on Peenemünde and the He 177, see *Revenge!* on page 92.)

Falling under gravity, the Fritz reached a terminal velocity of close to the speed of sound, making it very suitable for attacks on heavily-armoured warships. To achieve this, the PC-1400X's delivery profile required an overflight of the target at around 20,000ft (6,096m). After release, the pilot throttled back and lowered the flaps to enable the bomb aimer to keep the flare in sight and guide it to impact.

After further trials the Do 217K-2 – with its wingspan extended by 19ft and uprated BMW 801G engines – became the favoured ➤

Clockwise from far left Having penetrated deep into the hull the Fritz X ignited the forward magazine with devastating results.

'Roma', flagship of the surrendering Italian fleet, on September 9, 1943. BOTH MARINA MILITARE

The Fritz X was a devastating weapon against even the most heavily armoured warships. USAF

Hptm Bernhard Jope, commander of III/KG 100, in early September 1943. VIA JOHN WEAL

A Marauder of 14 Squadron flying past the 'Vittorio Veneto', the only battleship to escape the carnage of September 9.
GIL GRAHAM VIA M NAPIER

Right
A Baltimore IIIA of 52 Squadron, flown by Sqn Ldr Riddell, providing escort to the 'Roma' on the morning of September 9, 1943.
52 SQUADRON RECORDS

Below
Dornier Do 217K-2s of III/KG 100 on standby at Istres, early 1943.
BERNHARD JOPE

launch platform for Fritz X. Extremely slow production at the Rheinmetall factory meant that by mid-May 1943 just 100 bombs were available. Nonetheless, by the beginning of July, III Gruppe, Kampfgeschwader 100 Wiking (III/KG 100) moved to Istres on the French Mediterranean coast in readiness for operations.

ANTI SHIPPING 'ACE'
Reformed at Schwäbisch Hall in southern Germany on April 29, 1943,

III/KG 100 was initially led by Hptm Ernst Hetzel. On July 28 he handed the reins to Hptm Bernhard Jope, a 30-year-old who had joined the Luftwaffe in April 1935 and at the start of the war was flying Focke-Wulf Fw 200 Condors.

Jope gained fame (or notoriety) when, on October 26, 1940, to the north-west of Ireland he attacked and severely damaged the 42,350-ton troop transport RMS *Empress of Britain* which was finished off by a U-boat. The *Empress* was the largest

liner lost during World War Two and the largest victim of a German submarine.

With a technical background – he studied aeronautical engineering in university – and his experience in anti-shipping tactics, Jope was the ideal man to oversee the debut of the new weapon. Some attacks were flown against naval targets off Palermo, Syracuse and other ports. An unsuccessful strike on Allied shipping in the Straits of Messina on September 5 cost the Gruppe 'K-2 '6N+CD' and its crew. The bomber fell victim to a Spitfire of 154 Squadron flown by Rhodesian Flt Lt William Maguire, the ninth of his 13 victories.

UNDER A BLACK FLAG
In conditions of great secrecy an armistice between the Italians and the Allies had been signed at Cassibile on September 3. One clause stipulated

"After further trials the Do 217K-2 – with its wingspan extended by 19ft and uprated BMW 801G engines – became the favoured launch platform for Fritz X."

the surrender of the surface units of the Regia Marina.

Soon afterwards, the Gruppe was placed on standby and, as is the way of fighting men, rumours abounded as to what was going on. Only Jope knew the real answer; he had been ordered to Rome on the 7th where Generalfeldmarschall Wolfram von Richthofen of Luftflotte 2 ordered him to prepare for an attack on the Italian naval base at La Spezia.

Back at Istres, the Do 217K-2s of III/KG 100 were fuelled and loaded with a single light-blue Fritz X beneath their starboard wings. The crews awaited the call.

On the evening of September 8, Marshal Pietro Badoglio, the new Italian prime minister, announced the armistice. At 03:00 hours the next morning the fleet sailed from La Spezia bound for Malta.

It was a substantial force comprising the modern battleships *Vittorio Veneto*, *Italia* and *Roma*, the cruisers *Eugenio di Savoia*, *Raimondo Montecuccoli*, *Emanuele Filiberto Duca d'Aosta* and eight destroyers (*Legionario*, *Grecale*, *Oriani*, *Velite*, *Mitragliere*, *Fuciliere*, *Artigliere* and *Carabiniere*). En route three Genoa-based cruisers, *Duca degli Abruzzi*, *Giuseppe Garibaldi* and *Attilio Regolo*, joined the force. All were under the command of Admiral Carlo Bergamini, aboard the *Roma*.

As part of the agreement the ships of the Italian fleet were required to fly a black flag and were to be escorted by Allied aircraft. As dawn broke, Martin Baltimores of 52 Squadron and Martin Marauders of 14 Squadron from Protville in Tunisia took station near them. Soon afterwards Vizeadmiral Wilhelm Meendsen-Bohlken sent a signal to Berlin: "The Italian fleet has departed during the night to surrender itself to the enemy."

A FEW DEADLY MINUTES

As Istres, Jope rapidly briefed his astonished crews and at 14:00 led eleven Dorniers to find the defecting Italians. He reasoned that to avoid the Luftwaffe bases in southern Italy the fleet would route down the west coast of Corsica, an assumption that proved to be accurate.

In a clear sky the Dorniers began a slow climb in a loose formation to 20,000ft. Ninety minutes later, as their crews scanned the sea in almost unlimited visibility, they spotted the tell-tale wakes and set up for an attack on their erstwhile allies.

With the convoy 14 miles (22.5km) off Cape Testa, the Dorniers opened out at 15:37 and began their attack. The ships began to manoeuvre independently and opened fire with anti-aircraft guns. Jope noted: "From so high up we could not recognise the

individual ships; we just picked upon the biggest we could see and each ran in to bomb that."

In Jope's aircraft, bomb aimer Uffz Klapproth steered the Fritz X down – it struck the *Roma* midships on the starboard side. The armour-piercing bomb penetrated clean through the hull, exploding beneath the keel and causing severe damage. Water began to flood the aft engine room and two boiler rooms, causing the inboard propellers to stop and a number of small electrical fires to break out. Losing power and with just two screws functioning, the *Roma's* speed reduced to 10 knots and it began to fall out of formation.

A few minutes later a Fritz X struck the *Italia* to starboard, just beneath the forward main turrets. She began to take on more than 1,000 tons of water.

Around 16:02, a second Fritz X, possibly dropped from the Dornier piloted by Hptm Heinrich Schmetz and steered by his observer, Uffz Degan, slammed into the *Roma's* starboard side, close to the 15in gun turret, detonating in the forward engine room.

Within seconds of the initial blast the massive turret, weighing 1,500 tons, was blown over the side as the battleship was rent by a huge explosion when the magazine detonated. A column of flames ➤

Above
Fritz X-armed Do 217K-2s of III/KG 100 over the Mediterranean in early September 1943.
BERNHARD JOPE

Top
The crew of a Do 217
missile carrier, caught
baling out by the camera-
gun of 72 Squadron's Fg
Off Roy Hussey.
R D SCRASE

Above
KG 100's badge.

and smoke rose some 3,000ft over the stricken vessel.

As the fireball and smoke cleared, *Roma* was revealed as still afloat, but clearly her end was near. The battleship began to go down by the bow while listing more and more to starboard before capsizing, quickly breaking in two and sinking at 16:12. Of her crew of 1,849, only 596 were rescued. The remaining 1,253 – including Admiral Bergamini and *Roma's* captain, Adone del Cima – went down with her, victims of the deadly effectiveness of Jope's Dorniers with their new weapon.

Aboard *Italia*, Commandante Garofalo described the attack: "All this took place in a few minutes but we were now a long way from the point at which the *Roma* is halted and covered in smoke. The bows are almost invisible. The last vision I have of the flagship on which the day previously I have spent many hours are three flashes – like salutes – which rise up towards the sky, exploding in three red stars.

"The last voice which reached us is that of a radio-operator which says 'I am in danger'. This repeats after a second or two: 'I am in danger of death.'"

VIEW FROM ABOVE

The catastrophe was witnessed by the escorting Marauder flown by 14 Squadron's CO, Wg Cdr Law-Wright. He described it to an American journalist afterwards: "The first sign of attack we saw was

when the ships opened fire. For a moment we thought they were firing at us and we took violent evasive action. Then we saw flak burst far above us, obviously aimed at high-flying aircraft.

"We saw an enormous explosion on one of the battleships. Creamy white smoke went up to about 3,000 or 4,000ft. The smoke on the battleship subsided and it looked as if it were getting under way again. Throughout the attack the ships had taken excellent evasive action and their anti-aircraft fire was accurate.

"We flew over the ships and took a look at the damaged one. We arrived just as it was sinking. Under a big column of smoke we saw the stern under water and the bow sticking up. The ship appeared to break in two and folded up with the control tower and keel forming a 'V' as the ship slowly disappeared."

By then the Dorniers were heading for home, as Jope later recalled: "We did not see the *Roma* explode. That happened after we left. We saw the explosions as the bombs hit, sure, but how often have we seen this before and then the ship managed to limp back to port?"

Later in the day, the crews of III/KG 100 picked up the news of their incredible success on an Allied radio broadcast.

The cruiser *Attilio Regolo*, three destroyers and an escort vessel began rescuing the survivors of the *Roma* before heading to Port Mahon on the island of Menorca. Shocked by the catastrophe the remainder of the Italian fleet sailed for Malta.

After rendezvous with the Royal Navy, they were led to port by the battleship HMS *Warspite*.

On arrival, Admiral Sir Andrew Cunningham sent the following message to London: "Please to inform your Lordships that the Italian battle fleet now lies at anchor under the guns of the fortress of Malta."

MORE VICTIMS

The day after this stunning success Jope was promoted to Major and became the Geschwaderkommodore of KG 100, passing command of III Gruppe to Hptm Gerhard Döhler. The Gruppe's Dorniers mounted further attacks on Allied shipping supporting the landings at Salerno to the south of Naples where, despite Allied air superiority, they caused significant damage.

On September 11 a guided bomb struck the cruiser USS *Savannah*, the weapon penetrating the ship's 6in gun turret and causing major damage while a near miss by another Fritz X damaged the USS *Philadelphia*.

Further attacks two days later inadvertently sank the hospital ship *Newfoundland* with great loss of life. Other Dornier crews hit and damaged the cruiser HMS *Uganda* and the destroyers HMS *Loyal* and *Nubian*, albeit for the loss of four bombers to the increasing effective Allied defences.

Major success came on the 16th when Royal Navy battleships providing bombardment support off Salerno were attacked with Fritz X

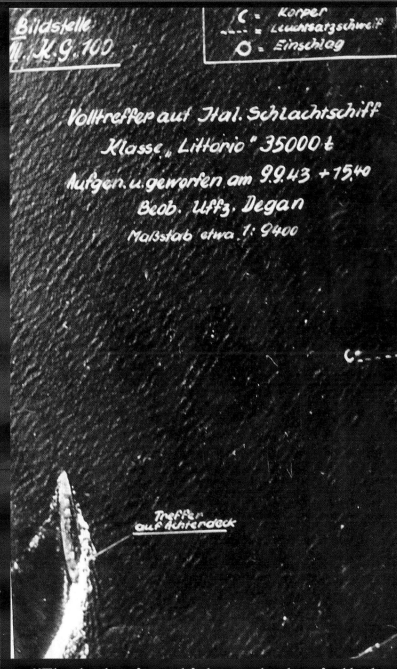

Bildstelle
III. K.G. 100

C = Körper
Leuchtsatzschweif
O = Einschlag

Volltreffer auf Ital. Schlachtschiff
Klasse „Littorio" 35000 t
Aufgen. u. geworfen am 9.9.43 +15.40
Beob. Uffz. Degan
Maßstab etwa 1: 9400

Treffer
auf Achterdeck

"The last voice which reached us is that of a radio-operator which says 'I am in danger'. This repeats after a second or two: 'I am in danger of death.'"

weapons. HMS *Valiant* was lightly damaged by a near miss, but her sister ship *Warspite* was not so lucky. She was hit three times one near her funnel, ripping through *six* decks before exploding against her double hull, blowing a hole in the bottom of the ship.

Fortunately no fire broke out, but *Warspite* had no steam and had shipped 5,000 tons of water. She had to be towed to Malta for emergency repairs.

Flying on patrol above were escorting Spitfires, including that flown by Fg Off Alan Peart of 81 Squadron. He thought the ship had been struck by a torpedo, but saw no sign of any torpedo-bombers, as he recalled: "We looked around for a different cause and sighted three Dornier Do 217s making their escape north up the coast. I felt it was a fine effort by these three Germans and wished them luck to survive following such a brave and audacious attack."

All this damage came at a cost to KG 100 and, over Salerno on the 20th, Fg Off Roy Hussey, flying a Spitfire of 72 Squadron, shot down a brace of Do 217s. Hussey's No.2, Plt Off Rodney Scrase, recalled: "I had trouble with my second-stage supercharger, which kept cutting in and out. Roy flew on ahead and shot down the first Dornier.

"By that time I had sorted out my problems; he had caught up with the second aircraft and got that one too. As I came up alongside the crew were baling out, but the last, who was in too much of a hurry to pull his ripcord, went down with his plane, the parachute see-sawing up and down the tailplane."

At then end of the month KG 100's guided bombs sank two tank-landing ships, LST 79 and LST 2231, in Ajaccio harbour, bringing the unit's period of stunning success to an end. The fortunes of III Gruppe had reached its zenith and it was soon withdrawn to Germany.

Bernhard Jope survived the war and, after a period in captivity, returned to flying as a pilot with Lufthansa, remaining with the airline until his retirement. He passed away at Königstein on July 31, 1995.

Seventeen years later, on June 28, 2012, the wreck of the *Roma* was found by an Italian submersible off the northern coast of Sardinia – a tragic hulk, a lasting reminder of a pioneering form of attack. ✠

Left
An original strike photograph showing the 'Roma' having been hit by Jope's bomb (marked 'Treffer') with the second, and fatal, missile inbound as indicated with the hook and dotted line. BERNHARD JOPE

Below left
The observer of a Dornier Do 217K-2 guiding a Fritz X missile onto its target. VIA ALFRED PRICE

DORNIER
Do 17

5K+HR

Dornier Do 17Z-2 '5K+HR' of KG 3,
Eastern Front, 1941. *PETE WEST © 2014*

BIG BROTHER

Dornier Do 217M-1 56158 was evaluated by Captain Eric Brown at the Royal Aircraft
Establishment, Farnborough, in October 1945. It was this machine he was describing in
his quote. *KEY COLLECTION*

Lessons learned from the Do 17 and the Do
215 produced an all-new growth version,
the Do 217. The prototype Do 217 V1 was
powered by Daimler-Benz DB.601As and
first flew in August 1938. From the start,
the type suffered from stability problems,
which delayed its entry into service. In
early 1940 the first recce-configured Do
217A-0s, powered by BMW 801 radials,
became operational. The Do 217 was
used for many operational purposes, the
bomber evolving into the Do 217K from
1942, with an all-glazed rounded nose.
Around 1,700 Do 217s were built.

Do 17E-1s of KG 255 exercising in 1938.

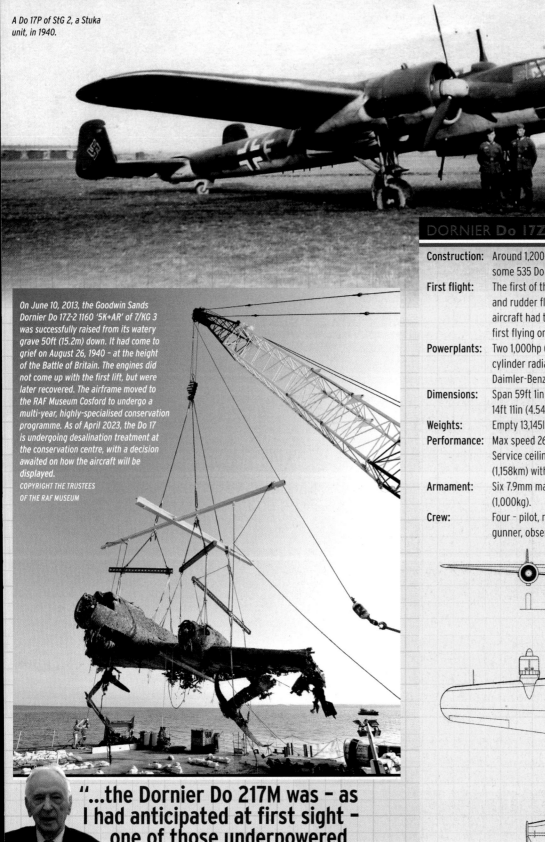

A Do 17P of StG 2, a Stuka unit, in 1940.

On June 10, 2013, the Goodwin Sands Dornier Do 17Z-2 1160 '5K+AR' of 7/KG 3 was successfully raised from its watery grave 50ft (15.2m) down. It had come to grief on August 26, 1940 – at the height of the Battle of Britain. The engines did not come up with the first lift, but were later recovered. The airframe moved to the RAF Museum Cosford to undergo a multi-year, highly-specialised conservation programme. As of April 2023, the Do 17 is undergoing desalination treatment at the conservation centre, with a decision awaited on how the aircraft will be displayed.

DORNIER Do 17Z-2

Construction:	Around 1,200 of all variants were built including some 535 Do 17Zs and 112 Do 215s.
First flight:	The first of three Do 17 prototypes with single fin and rudder flew on November 23, 1934. Subsequent aircraft had the more familiar twin-fin design, the first flying on May 18, 1935.
Powerplants:	Two 1,000hp (746kW) Bramo Fafnir 323P nine-cylinder radials. The Do 215 had two 1,100hp Daimler-Benz DB601A inverted V12 units.
Dimensions:	Span 59ft 1in (18m) Length 51ft 9in (15.77m) Height 14ft 11in (4.54m) Wing area 592ft² (55m²)
Weights:	Empty 13,145lb (5,962kg). Loaded 18,937lb (8,589kg).
Performance:	Max speed 263mph (423km/h) at 16,400ft (5,000m). Service ceiling 26,740ft (8,150m). Range 720 miles (1,158km) with 1,100lb bomb load.
Armament:	Six 7.9mm machine-guns. Max bomb load 2,205lb (1,000kg).
Crew:	Four – pilot, radio operator/gunner, bombardier/gunner, observer/gunner.

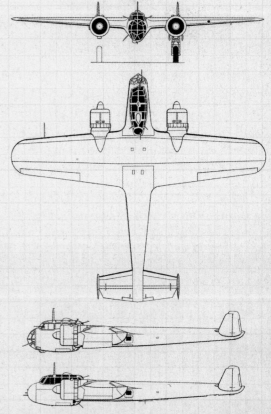

"...the Dornier Do 217M was – as I had anticipated at first sight – one of those underpowered twins that abounded in the early 1940s timescale; it had certainly been less lethal than some of them and at least pleasant to fly when everything was working!"

CAPTAIN ERIC 'WINKLE' BROWN - SEE PAGE 97

Dornier Do 17Z-2 with, at the bottom, a Do 17Z-7. KEY COLLECTION

JUNKERS
Ju 52

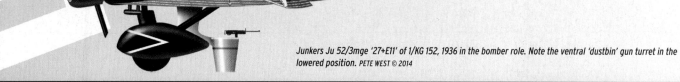

Junkers Ju 52/3mge '27+E11' of 1/KG 152, 1936 in the bomber role. Note the ventral 'dustbin' gun turret in the lowered position. PETE WEST © 2014

FOR 'JUNKERS' READ 'JUPITER'

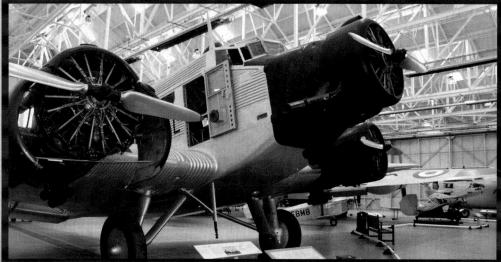

Heads usually turn as visitors to the RAF Museum Cosford pass the silver and black 'Tante Ju' in Hangar 1. It's the title 'British Airways' that tends to stop them in their tracks. The former Spanish Air Force 1954-built CASA 352L is painted to represent a Ju 52/3mge delivered to the *first* airline to be called British Airways, at Croydon in early 1938.

Further reading of the placard reveals that post-war, British European Airways used a fleet of former Luftwaffe Ju 52s that were refurbished for airline used by Short Brothers at Sydenham, Belfast. Named the Jupiter-class, the tri-motors served with BEA from late 1946 until early 1948.

During the invasion of Norway in early April 1940 massed fleets of Ju 52s dropping paratroops and re-supplying were vital to the operation. Many examples were lost, including Ju 523mge 6657 'CA+JY' of 3/KGzbV 102 which crash landed into Lake Hartvigvannet on April 13. (KGzbV - Kampfgeschwader zur besonderen Verwendung – special-purpose bomber unit.) It was salvaged during the summer of 1983 – note the additional machine-gun position over the cockpit. Restored, 'CA+JY' is now on display at the Royal Norwegian Air Force Museum at Gardermoen, Oslo. KEY COLLECTION

A tiny number of airworthy Ju52s remain globally, with several others on static display. Thanks to their longevity of operation, many are from the batch built post-war in Spain by CASA. Illustrated while serving with the Commemorative Air Force, Pratt & Whitney R1340-engined N352JU, a former Spanish Air Force CASA 352L. It wears the colours of '1Z+AR' of Stab IV/KGzbV which took part in the invasion of Crete, Operation MERKUR, in May 1941. *KEY-DUNCAN CUBITT*

"I discovered the very real affection for the 'Tante Ju' (Auntie Junkers) possessed by the Wehrmacht as a whole, and began to appreciate the fact that this transport had probably played a greater role in shaping the course of World War Two than any combat aeroplane."

CAPTAIN ERIC 'WINKLE' BROWN - SEE PAGE 97

JUNKERS Ju 52/3mg3e

Construction:	Built initially as an airliner, then series production for the Luftwaffe; the last wartime deliveries being made in mid-1944. Also built by Amiot in France from 1941. Post-war Amiot built 415 as the AAC.1 Toucan, and CASA in Spain built 166 CASA 352s up to the mid-1950s. Total production came to just over 5,400 units.
First Flight:	October 13, 1930 as a single-engined transport, powered by an 800hp (596kW) Junkers L88 12-cylinder 'vee' piston engine. Redesigned, it first flew in its three-engined format in April 1932 – hence the /3mg (tri-motor) suffix to the designation.
Powerplant:	Three 725hp (540kW) BMW 132A-3 radial piston engines.
Dimensions:	Span 95ft 11½in (29.24m) Length 62ft 0in (18.89m) Height 18ft 2½in (5.54m) Wing area 1,189ft² (110.45m²).
Weights:	Empty 12,610lb (5,719kg) Max all-up 23,146lb (10,499kg).
Performance:	Max speed 165mph (265km/h) at sea level. Service ceiling 19,360ft (5,900m) Typical range 620 miles (997km).
Armament:	Bomber mode: One 7.9mm machine-gin in dorsal position, one 7.9mm machine-gun in semi-retractable ventral 'dustbin' turret. Up to 1,100lb (498kg) of bombs. Transport role: One 7.9mm machine-gin in dorsal position.
Crew:	Four/Five. Accommodation for up to 24 paratroops.

A leaping stag on the nose of a KGzbV 105 'Tante Ju'.

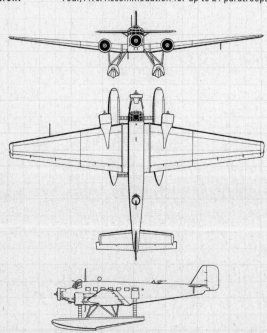

Junkers Ju 52/3mg5e floatplane. Note the additional gun position in the top of the cockpit; the gunner standing in between the pilots. *KEY COLLECTION*

NEW YEAR'S DAY AT EINDHOVEN

Firing away with a pistol at the Luftwaffe fighters, even though the Typhoon he was using for cover was ablaze, Plt Off Andy Lord of 438 Squadron RCAF got a dramatic view of JG 3's spectacular raid on B78, Eindhoven. Having had his aircraft disabled, he was so mad that he climbed down from the cockpit and retaliated with the only weapon he had. Quickly, common sense prevailed and he took cover in an old bomb crater.

Andy - centre foreground at the tail of *G-for-George* - commissioned aviation historian and artist Chris Thomas to create the incredible painting that starts our BODENPLATTE feature. Chris depicted the airfield at 09:25 hours on New Year's Day. The layout was based on an aerial photo taken three days after the attack. All of the pilots of the Typhoons in the foreground survived; Chris managed to trace three of them and their descriptions helped in creating the scene.

On the right, the Typhoons of 440 Squadron RCAF are shown taxying out to the runway; they were also badly shot up. Within the line-up, Plt Off Dick Watson of 440 Squadron RCAF - who Chris also spoke to - has turned his aircraft, hit the brakes and throttle to raised the tail so that he could momentarily shoot at an Fw 190 at *very* low level. Dick claimed it as damaged, but it was not awarded to him.

To the left, the B-17 Fortress was under repair, having 'lobbed in' with mechanical troubles: it was destroyed. In the left background, the PR Spitfires on the cross runway were receiving a heavy mauling. At the extreme left is a mushroom-like cloud as the bomb dump erupts.

In the air, Major Heinz Bär, JG 3's 'boss' is screaming through in Fw 190 *Red 13* (left, foreground). He had just shot down two Typhoons (claiming them as Tempests), his 204th and 205th victories. In the centre, mid-ground, Flt Lt H P Gibbons in Typhoon *D-for-Dog* is moments from shooting the tail off an Fw 190. Tragically, behind him are Bf 109s queuing up to shoot him down; he was killed defending his base.

CHRIS THOMAS © 2014

WAKE UP *Call*

IT COULD HAVE BEEN A CATACLYSMIC BLOW TO THE ALLIED ADVANCE. INSTEAD, THE LUFTWAFFE'S NEW YEAR'S DAY RE-INVENTION OF BLITZKRIEG WAS A COSTLY, BUT HEROIC, VENTURE. **CHRIS GOSS** EXPLAINS ➤

pulling its weight; the scale of effort was low and attacks were not pressed home.

"Results were so poor that Hitler had been hinting that the Luftwaffe would do better in the infantry. This state of affairs must change - new aircraft were coming off the assembly lines in thousands and thousands (banging his hand on the table each time he said 'thousand' for effect) and the Luftwaffe must now justify its existence and produce operations on a large scale…"

Whether this is *exactly* what happened cannot be ascertained for sure, but what *can* be said for certain is that just after dawn on New Year's Day 1945, German fighters launched en masse and headed towards Allied airfields in France, Belgium and Holland. They were intent on

destroying as many Allied aircraft as possible, Operation BODENPLATTE had begun.

[Bodenplatte literally translates as 'base plate', as in the substantial structure at the bottom of a mortar tube. Perhaps a more vivid interpretation would be 'launch pad' – ED.]

As early as November 14, Göring issued orders for BODENPLATTE. There were four aims in support of what was hoped to be a ground offensive westwards: To hit allied fighter-bombers at their bases near the front line; provide fighter cover for the German army; Luftwaffe fighter-bombers to support the crossing of the River Meuse; attacks on Allied airfields to be carried out by jet bombers while non-jet types and night-fighters would strike at other targets.

A summons to Berlin to attend a meeting with Reichsmarschall Hermann Göring was bound to get his attention. It was early in November 1944 and Oberstleutnant Johann Kogler, the Austrian Geschwader Kommodore of Jagdgeschwader JG 6, made haste. He was not the only executive officer present; most of the Jagdgeschwadern on the western front were represented.

Kogler later reported: "The great man cracked the whip with some vigour. His Luftwaffe had not been

"Results were so poor that Hitler had been hinting that the Luftwaffe would do better in the infantry. This state of affairs must change... and the Luftwaffe must now justify its existence and produce operations on a large scale..."

WAITING FOR THE WORD

Preparations were complete by the start of December 1944, but all had to be put on hold until the weather improved. Detailed planning included transferring Junkers Ju 88s from various Nachtjadgeschwadern to act as 'pathfinders' for the single-engined fighters.

Meanwhile, the Allies had to contend with Generalfeldmarschall Gerd von Rundstedt's ground

offensive, otherwise known as the 'Battle of the Bulge'. The poor weather limited the effectiveness of their aircraft, but was equally hampering Germany's effort. Luftwaffe unit commanders waited for the signal to put the grand plan into action.

At about 18:30 hours on New Year's Eve 1944, the code word HERMANN was given, together with the date and time: 09:20 on January 1, 1945.

FIRST BLOOD

The massed formations lifted off from airfields in western Germany and eastern Holland. Led by their night-fighter pathfinders, the armada headed for its targets – see panel.

The Allies did not have to wait long for what are believed to be the first air-to-air losses. At 08:29, two Spitfires from 2 Squadron, flown by Flt Lts J M Young and L J Packwood, took off from Gilze-Rijen in Holland to recce the Leeuwen-Hilversum-Arnhem area. East of Amersfoort at 09:05, the two pilots spotted two Ju 88s, apparently escorted by a mixed bunch of Messerschmitt Bf 109s and Focke-Wulf Fw 190s.

Packwood reported: "I attacked a Me 109 from dead astern and above, the enemy aircraft took no evasive action. I gave it a five-second burst with cannon and machine-guns, closing from 400 to 150 yards...

the enemy aircraft disintegrated, the starboard wing broke off and flicked over on its back and hit the ground in flames…" His victim was Unteroffizier (Uffz) Heinrich Braun of 2/JG 27, who was headed towards Brussels-Melsbroek.

As this was taking place, a pair of 268 Squadron Mustangs, flown by Flt Lts Dave Mercer and J B Lyke, also out of Gilze-Rijen on a similar recce, spotted what they thought were three Ju *188*s and five Bf 109s over Utrecht. They were actually Ju 88s, which had carried out their pathfinding task and were returning with 'lame ducks'.

In a short, sharp combat, the Ju 88G-1 of 5/NJG 1 flown by Uffz Wilhelm Fischer, plunged into a wood near the Dutch village of Barneveld at 09:15 hours, killing all four crew. The first of many deaths that day had occurred.

IT'S NOT APRIL 1!

Led by its inspirational Kommodore, Oberst Herbert Ihlefeld, Jagdgeschwader (JG) 1 got airborne from its bases at Twente/Enschede, Rheine and Drope just before 08:15, bound for Maldeghem, Ursel and St Denis-Westrem in Belgium. Flying between 160 and 320ft (50 and 100m), the omens were not good – 'friendly fire' accounted for three Fw 190s. Herbert Ihlefeld was also hit by flak, but successfully crash-landed at Rotterdam.

Meanwhile, the lead Ju 88 for III/ JG 1, flown by Leutnant (Lt) Josef ➤

Above
A pair of GIs inspect the Fw 190D-9 of Fw Werner Hohenberg of JG 2 just southeast of Aachen.

Below left
Ofhr Franz Schaar, one of the victims of JG 4 in 'White 16', a Sturm Fw 190.

LUFTWAFFE UNITS AND **TARGET AIRFIELDS**

JG 1:	Maldeghem (B65), Ursel (B67), St Denis-Westrem (B61), Belgium
JG 2	St Trond (A92), Belgium
JG 3	Eindhoven (B78), Holland
JG 4	Le Culot (B68), Belgium
JG 6	Volkel (B80), Holland
JG 11	Asch (Y29), Belgium
JG 26	Grimbergen (B60) and Brussels-Evere (B56), Belgium
JG 27	Brussels-Melsbroek (B58), Belgium
JG 53	Étain (A82) and Metz-Frescaty (Y34), France
III/JG 54	Grimbergen (B60), Belgium
IV/JG 54	Brussels-Melsbroek (B58), Belgium
JG 77	Antwerp-Deurne (B70), Belgium
SG 4	St Trond (A92), Belgium
KG 51	Gilze-Rijen (B77), Volkel (B80) and Eindhoven (B78), Holland
III/KG 76	Gilze-Rijen (B77), Holland

Note: Letters and numbers refer to Allied airfield designations.

Below
Brussels-Melsbroek, a Wellington from 69 Squadron on fire.

Hettlich of 9/NJG 1 was also shot down by German flak, as was the replacement flown by Uffz Ingomar Mayr!

The fighters' approach had not gone unnoticed as Sqn Ldr G Dickinson, based on the Belgian coast at Knocke, wrote: "...a vast swarm of Fw 190s and Me 109s swept across... My efforts to explain the position to the Duty Ops Officer were to no avail. Jovially, he insisted on wishing me a happy New Year, reminding me that 'This is January 1 old boy, not April 1!' Then I heard a strangled cry: 'The bastards are here!' and that was the last we heard from group HQ for some time!"

The attack on Maldeghem is best summed up by Oberfaehnrich Wilhelm Ade of 2/JG 1: "I was already over the airfield before I could react. We banked and went in. I remember

seeing about three four-engine bombers. Together with my Staffel, I followed the others...

"Stupidly enough, we still had to maintain radio silence and therefore could not give any instructions. We simply had to assume that the others did the same as we did. [I] do not understand why we had to maintain radio silence over the target – they knew we were there, so what was the point?

"Strafing the airfield, I fired at the parked aircraft, achieved hits at some of them and pulled up again... It seemed that we also flew over St Denis-Westrem [airfield]. Suddenly someone broke radio silence and shouted: 'Spitfires!'"

By luck, 308 and 317 Squadrons were returning to St Denis-Westrem from an armed recce and waded into the German fighters; claiming 19 destroyed, one 'probable' and five damaged. The total cost to JG 1 was 29 fighters shot down and four damaged. Of the 24 Luftwaffe pilots who did not return, seven were taken prisoner, one evaded capture.

Allied losses were 54 aircraft on the ground, two Spitfires in the air and a further seven damaged in forced landings. As with many of the other BODENPLATTE attacks, the results did not justify the cost to the Luftwaffe.

MURDEROUS BARRAGE
The strike on St Trond in Belgium was carried out by two Geschwadern – Oberstleutnant Kurt Bühligen's Richthofen Geschwader, JG 2, and Oberst Alfred Druschel's ground-attack SG 4. St Trond was the home to P-47 Thunderbolts of the 48th and 404th Fighter Groups (FG) of the USAAF's Ninth Air Force.

Being so close to the front line, the

base had considerable anti-aircraft defences and the Germans flew into a murderous barrage. JG 2 suffered 43 fighters destroyed and 12 damaged. Half of JG 2's attacking force was lost to flak, mainly because the route taken was over a battle zone!

As for SG 4, it never really played a part as the Geschwader failed to form up. Only a handful of aircraft participated; four were shot down including SG 4's Oberst Druschel, who simply disappeared.

The cost to the Americans at St Trond was fewer than 20 aircraft destroyed and numerous others damaged.

SITTING DUCKS
Commanded by the highly experienced Major Heinz Bär, JG 3 was one of the most easterly of the Jagdgeschwadern. Its pilots had to run the gauntlet of their own as well as Allied flak, but lost just two aircraft on the run in on what became the most successful raid that day.

Based at JG 3's target, Eindhoven in Holland, Plt Off John Colton from 137 Squadron remembered: "The attack started at about 09:20 hours with most of us trying to get over our New Year's Eve party. You never saw so many land-locked pilots shooting at low-flying '109s and '190s flying over our living quarters.

"We did have one flight airborne a recce when the raid started and this was when Plt Off Lance Burrows got shot on the runway whilst taxiing... As it happened, the raid started just as he landed and was rolling off the runway when he was hit. Never had a chance..."

No.137 was not the only squadron caught unawares by JG 3 - Typhoons of 438 and 440 Squadrons RCAF, taxiing out, were 'sitting ducks'.

Likewise the sole Typhoon from 168 Squadron that accounted for an Fw 190 before itself being shot down. Two of the Typhoons were claimed by Major Bär. During the attack JG 3 was joined by elements of I/JG 6, which mistakenly attacked Eindhoven instead of Volkel.

Damage at Eindhoven has been hard to quantify, but *at least* 44 Allied aircraft had been destroyed and in the region of 60 damaged. Fifteen personnel were killed and more than 40 wounded. The Luftwaffe suffered 15 fighters lost and three damaged; nine pilots killed and six prisoners of war.

"It seems clear that the navigation – allegedly that of the Ju 88 – was faulty and that the southward turn was made at a point too far west. In any case, it is patent that the unit as a whole failed to find Volkel – though one or two individuals may have done so... this attack was a conspicuous failure."

Kogler was shot down by flak and was taken prisoner before any airfield was raided. I/JG 6 mistakenly hit Eindhoven, albeit with some success, while the remainder of the Geschwader blundered around looking for Volkel. They over-flew the airfield at Heesch and the based

352nd FG the chance to take-off.

In the massive dogfight that followed, joined by Spitfires of 610 Squadron, the Americans claimed to have shot down 33 Germans. In reality, JG 11 lost 24 aircraft, but just four pilots were taken prisoner. One of those who perished was Specht – yet another hard blow for the Luftwaffe's already depleted 'stock' of experienced men.

Above
Lt Siegfried Müller, Staffelführer of 16/JG 3 who led all of JG 3 to Eindhoven.

Left
Ofw Franz Meindl in front of his Fw 190 in 1943. This experienced pilot, with 31 victories, was killed in the battle of Asch with 8/JG 11.

"...a vast swarm of Fw 190s and Me 109s swept across... My efforts to explain the position to the Duty Ops Officer were to no avail. Jovially, he insisted on wishing me a happy New Year, reminding me that 'This is January 1 old boy, not April 1!'

CONSPICUOUS FAILURE
The attack by JG 4 on another Ninth Air Force base, Le Culot in Belgium, was a total failure. Of the 75 fighters assigned, just 12 reached an airfield. Losses amounted to 26 aircraft and a further six were damaged – almost half of the force failed to return. Even two of the pathfinder Ju 88s did not make it back.

Commanded by Oberst Johann Kogler, JG 6 had been in existence only four months, two of its Gruppen having converted from Me 410s to Fw 190s. Despite a number of experienced single-engined fighter pilots on its strength, luck seems to have avoided this Geschwader. Bad fortune continued during its mission to the Dutch base at Volkel, as the intelligence report noted:

Spitfires 'bounced' the German fighters, which eventually struck at Helmond airfield.

The cost to the Luftwaffe was 28 aircraft shot down, numerous damaged, 16 pilots killed or missing and seven taken prisoner. A few days later, the severely depleted JG 6 was withdrawn from operations.

Intense ground fire quickly accounted for a number of Major Günther Specht's JG 11 fighters as it attacked the Belgian airfield at Asch. Some attacked the wrong objective – Ophoven, very close to Asch and the home to four Spitfire squadrons.

At Asch, eight P-47s of the 390th Fighter Squadron (FS) were already airborne and ideally situated to bounce the Germans. This gave a dozen P-51 Mustangs from the

NOBODY HOME
Unbeknown to the Luftwaffe, the RAF had vacated Grimbergen in Belgium the day before BODENPLATTE. The new squadrons, from 131 Wing, had not yet arrived, although the Wing CO, Gp Capt Gabszewicz, happened to be visiting when the Germans attacked.

Conducted by I/JG 26 and III/JG 54, the raid was doomed from the start, a number of fighters went down to both 'friendly' and unfriendly flak before they were anywhere near the target. While the force was overhead, anti-aircraft fire and Spitfires from 308 Squadron accounted for yet more Luftwaffe fighters.

At 'empty' Grimbergen, the Germans lost 21 aircraft and 17 pilots, of which eight became prisoners. Curiously, an ➤

Top
Groundcrew of 12/JG 53 warming up a Bf 109G-14 in January 1945.

Above
Polish airmen inspecting the engine of a downed Fw 190 near Gent.

Above right
One of the many victims of JG 3 at Eindhoven, Spitfire PR.XI PA894 of 400 Squadron.

Fw 190D-9 flown by Lt Theo Nibel was downed, not by gunfire, but by a partridge holing his radiator!

TAKING A PASTING

Unlike Grimbergen, at Evere, close to the centre of Brussels, targets were plentiful. The Luftwaffe's intentions had already been transmitted to Evere by an Auster observation pilot who had flown head-on through one of the battle formations without incident.

Immediately before the German attack, two Spitfires were already airborne, another pair was on the runway just getting away and a further 12 had been called to readiness and were taxying out.

It was this dozen, from 416 Squadron RCAF, that had the misfortune to be bounced. Only Flt Lt Dave Harling took off, shot down a German fighter only to be pounced upon by another two; he was killed in the inevitable crash. Meanwhile, one of the Spitfires, which had got up earlier returned to the fray, closely joined by another two; the trio claimed eight fighters shot down.

Nevertheless, II and III/JG 26 remained over Evere for nearly 30 minutes. Around 60 aircraft of various types were either written off or damaged. German losses were 13 fighters of II/JG 26 destroyed, five pilots killed and four captured; III/JG 26: six fighters and four pilots. The successes at Evere were overshadowed by the debacle at Grimbergen.

SEA OF SMOKE AND FLAME

The attack on the Brussels airfield of Melsbroek was as spectacular as that on Evere; all kinds of Allied aircraft were there for the picking. Yet again, the approach to the target saw a number of German losses, either to enemy action or accidents. The formation arrived in fine style and after the third pass, Melsbroek was a sea of smoke and flame.

Neat parking by the resident Mitchell units resulted in carnage: 98 Squadron suffered four destroyed, 180 Squadron five and the Dutch 320 Squadron two. Eleven Wellingtons of 69 Squadron were demolished and two so badly damaged that they were written off.

All of 140 Squadron's Mosquitos were wiped out while 16 Squadron lost at least five Spitfires. A large number of visiting aircraft were on the ground that day – of these, at least 15 RAF and nearly 20 USAAF types were confined to scrap.

Flak accounted for most of the German failed-to-returns: JG 27 lost 17 aircraft, 11 pilots killed and three taken prisoner; IV/JG 54 three fighters, two pilots killed and one prisoner. While the Luftwaffe regarded these statistics as acceptable, the leader of III/JG 27 that day, Oberleutnant Emil Clade, later gave a more accurate analysis as he had: "... underestimated the potential of the Allies to replace the destroyed aircraft in a matter of days. They had suffered no personnel losses and in our case every loss counted. It would be one of the last heroic deeds of the Luftwaffe and now the last of us recognised that not even a miracle could save us..."

Little can be said about the failure by JG 77 to hit Deurne, near Antwerp. Only about half of the formation of 36 made it to the target. As one bystander wrote, when

JG 77 arrived they: "put up a very poor show".

The airfield was full of aircraft, but just six Typhoons were written off, the Luftwaffe preferring to concentrate on the larger types, destroying a B-17 and a Dakota. The Germans lost 11 fighters as well as two of the night-fighter leads; six pilots were killed, five became prisoners.

FRENCH TARGETS

JG 53 had fought with distinction in nearly every theatre of war. On January 1, 1945 its task was to hit the southernmost targets in north-eastern France: the Ninth Air Force bases at Étain and Metz-Frascaty. Unfortunately, 12 Thunderbolts from the 367th FS were on an armed recce when they spotted III/JG 53 headed towards Étain.

Jettisoning their bombs, the Americans went straight into combat; claiming 14 Messerschmitts destroyed, one 'probable' and many damaged, without a single loss to themselves. To make matters worse, the 366th FS pounced on the fleeing Germans, shooting down one and damaging four. One US pilot was shot down and taken prisoner. The 365th was not to be left out, downing one of the retiring lead Ju 88s and damaging another. Suffice to say, the assault on Étain was a total failure.

Meanwhile, the remainder of JG 53 were headed towards Metz-Frascaty. Yet again, American flak proved deadly for some of the attackers. Eventually IV/JG 53 made it to its target and for at least ten minutes proceeded to rake the airfield with gunfire.

The end result was 22 P-47s destroyed on the ground with another 11 damaged. However, JG 53 lost 30 fighters out of a total of 80; nine pilots were killed, four taken prisoner and six wounded. While JG 53's ability as a coherent combat unit was severely impaired; the Americans had replaced their losses within a week.

UNSCATHED JETS

Two more German units were involved on New Year's Day, the Messerschmitt Me 262-equipped KG 51 and III/KG 76 with Arado Ar 234s. It is thought that up to 19 Me 262s got airborne at some stage, apparently attacking airfields in Holland.

Six Ar 234 jet bombers from III/KG 76 probably struck at Gilze-Rijen. Both raids appear inconsequential, but at least all of the jets returned unscathed.

IRREPLACEABLE LOSSES

Loss figures for BODENPLATTE have been assessed as: German aircraft destroyed 280, damaged 69; Allied aircraft destroyed 232, damaged 156. Recent research on Allied losses indicates that these figures were conservative and just over 300 destroyed and 190 damaged would be more realistic.

However, the Allied war machine's ability to replace the aircraft was both quick and effective. For Germany it was much harder to redress the balance, thanks to the attrition being inflicted on both its industry and the Luftwaffe before and immediately after BODENPLATTE.

Impossible to replace were the German airmen: 168 pilots killed or missing, 73 taken prisoner and 24 wounded. Forty-five were regarded as experienced pilots and 21 executive-level officers – with skills that had taken years to acquire.

What of the ground offensive in the Ardennes, the Battle of the Bulge? Any effect that BODENPLATTE may have had was negated as by the New Year the advance westwards had ground to a halt.

Why did they do it? As Adolf Hitler said that same day: "The world must know that this state will therefore never capitulate... Germany will rise like a phoenix from its ruined cities and will go down again as the miracle of the 20th Century…"

Göring's re-invention of the Blitzkrieg had failed. The Ar 234s and Me 262s that had swept onto the stage provided a pointer for the future. The Reich as dependant on new technology for its revenge...

With many thanks to John Manrho for considerable help with the images used in this feature and his consent to quote several eyewitness accounts from his book. John is co-author, with the late Ron Putz, of the exceptional Bodenplatte – The Luftwaffe's Last Hope, published by Hikoki in 2004. If you can track down a copy, it is an incredible study of a momentous 24 hours. ✠

Below
Dark pillars of smoke rising above Y34 Metz.

"It would be one of the last heroic deeds of the Luftwaffe and now the last of us recognised that not even a miracle could save us..."

REVENGE *Weapons*

JONATHAN GARRAWAY PRESENTS A TIMELINE OF THE NEW AIRCRAFT AND WEAPONS THAT IT WAS HOPED WOULD SAVE THE THIRD REICH

Above
Often confused with the Luftwaffe's later weapons of war, the lumbering He 177 actually owed its origins to an RLM requirement of 1938.
KEY COLLECTION

Right
Perhaps the most famous of the V-weapons was the 'Doodlebug', although it was relatively 'low-tech' and counter-measures proved very effective.
PETE WEST © 2014

1936

German rocketry experiments started at Borkum, an island off the north west of the country, in 1934. The Heereswaffenamt (Army Ordnance Board) and the Reichsluftfahrtministerium (RLM – German Air Ministry) combined to acquire vast tracts of land at Peenemünde on the Baltic coast in **April 1936**, turning it into a test range and airfield complex. In December 1937, the 25ft (7.6m) A3 rocket was tested. This 'stood' on tail fins and was launched vertically – a configuration that was adopted by the world's first tactical ballistic missile, the V-2.

1939

Erich Warsitz took the tiny, wooden-winged Heinkel He 178 into the air from Marienehe, near Rostock, on **August 27, 1939**; the first-ever flight by a jet aircraft, propelled by a Heinkel-developed HeS 3b axial flow turbojet. (Frank Whittle's turbojet endeavours flew for the first time in the Gloster E28/39 on May 15, 1941.)The project was all the more remarkable as it was entirely a private venture. This breakthrough was initially greeted coolly by the authorities, but this soon altered.

Heinkel's huge He 177 Greif (Griffon) is often erroneously referred to as one the Third Reich's responses as the tide of war turned against it. Germany's only operational heavy bomber actually had its maiden voyage on **November 19**, 1939, in response to an RLM requirement of the previous year. With no piston engines available offering more than 2,000hp (1,492kW), a pair of Daimler-Benz DB 601s were coupled to a common drive shaft to produce 2,600hp, as the DB 606. Despite its looks, therefore, the He 177 was a *four-engined* aircraft.

That inaugural flight lasted only 12 minutes as the engines overheated. Powerplant and other problems continually plagued the He 177. Operational trials began in August 1941 and KG 40 raided Bristol using the type on August 28, 1942. By November 1943, the Greif had been adopted to carry Henschel Hs 293 anti-shipping missiles. The He 177 continued to fly into early 1945, but the aircraft never fulfilled its intended role as a heavy raid generator.

1941

Forty-three days before the British Gloster E28/39 jet fighter experimental flew, Heinkel's twin-jet He 280 had its maiden flight on **April 4, 1941**. Intended as a prototype fighter, this was a major milestone. Development continued into 1944, but by then the He 280 had been sidelined in favour of the Messerschmitt Me 262.

Surprisingly, **April 18** was the date of the first flight of the Me 262. Due to delays in obtaining suitable turbojets, the Me 262 V1 was powered by a 1,200hp (895kW) Jumo 210G *piston* engine, mounted in the nose.

Conceived as a point-defence fighter, the Me 163 Komet featured a swept-wing, tail-less format. A rocket motor which used a volatile fuel mixture, blasted it to height. It would then coast to its target and glide back to its base. The first glider flights took place at Lechfeld, in Bavaria, in the spring, before the prototype moved to Peenemünde for installation of the rocket motor.

> "Heine Dittmar lit the rocket on October 2 and achieved a world record speed of 623mph becoming the first man to travel at the 'magic' 1,000km/h."

Above
Members of the public inspecting one of the Third Reich's 'super weapons', an Me 163, post-war. KEC

Below
An operational Me 163B of JG400 – 'White 25' was captured at Husum, near Denmark, in 1945 and is now on display in Berlin.
PETE WEST © 2014

Towed to height behind a Messerschmitt Bf 110, Heine Dittmar lit the rocket on **October 2** and achieved a world record speed of 623mph, becoming the first man to travel at the 'magic' 1,000km/h. Despite the dangerous nature of the rocket motor and the practical problems of a fighter that turned into a glider for return to base, the dazzling performance of the Me 163 was too good to pass up.

By the end of 1941, Arado had substantially completed the Ar 234 V1 and V2 Blitz (Lightning) twin-bomber prototypes. They had to await flight-rated Jumo 004 turbojets.

1942
Fitted with Jumo 109-004 turbojets, the Me 262 V3 prototype got airborne on **July 18, 1942**. The programme faced many problems, including protracted engine development schedules, but it was destined to be the world's first operational jet fighter.

Radically redesigned and re-thought, the Me 163B point-defence fighter began flight tests in **August**. Production examples were fitted with a pair of 30mm cannon, capable of inflicting considerable damage on an Allied bomber, particularly if engaged

head-on. Erprobungskommando 16 (EKdo – proving detachment) was established at Peenemünde in February 1943 to build up a cadre of pilots and to evolve tactics.

On March 18, 1942 the first A4 rocket was statically tested at Peenemünde, but it exploded on the launch pad. By late 1942 the A4 was showing promise; it could propel a 2,150lb (975kg) warhead at 3,466mph (5,580km/h) close on 200 miles (321km) and be fired from mobile launchers. On **December 22** it was officially adopted ➤

191904

✠25

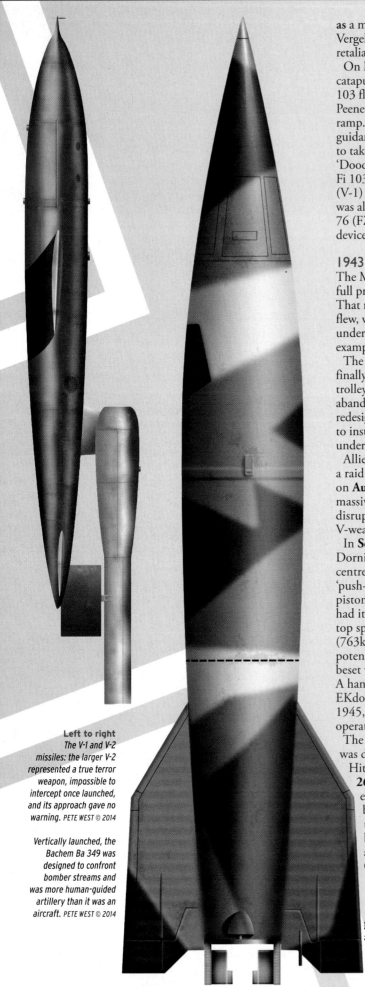

Left to right
The V-1 and V-2 missiles: the larger V-2 represented a true terror weapon, impossible to intercept once launched, and its approach gave no warning. PETE WEST © 2014

Vertically launched, the Bachem Ba 349 was designed to confront bomber streams and was more human-guided artillery than it was an aircraft. PETE WEST © 2014

as a major programme, becoming Vergeltungswaffe 2 (V-2 – revenge/ retaliation weapon No.2).

On **December 24**, the first catapult launch of a Fieseler Fi 103 flying-bomb took place at Peenemünde, from a 150ft (46m) ramp. Developing the flight profile, guidance and triggering systems was to take much more time, but the 'Doodlebug' had been born. The Fi 103 became Vergeltungswaffe 1 (V-1) but, for deception purposes, was also designated Flakzielgerät 76 (FZG-76 – anti-aircraft aiming device).

1943

The Me 262 was ordered into full production on **June 5, 1943**. That month the V6 prototype flew, with fully retractable tricycle undercarriage; the first four examples being 'taildraggers'.

The prototype Ar 234 twin-jet finally flew on **June 13**. Soon the trolley-launch system was abandoned and a major redesign was initiated to install retractable undercarriage.

Allied bombers staged a raid on Peenemünde on **August 17**, creating massive damage and disruption to the V-weapons programme.

In **September**, the Dornier Do 335 V1, centre-line thrust (or 'push-me, pull-you') piston-engined fighter had its debut. With a top speed of 474mph (763km/h) it showed potential, but was beset with problems. A handful reached EKdo 335 by March 1945, but none entered operational service.

The Me 262 V6 was demonstrated to Hitler on **November 26**. He was very enthusiastic, but saw it as the ultimate Schnell-bomber and not as an interceptor. Creating the Me 262A-2a Sturmvogel (Stormbird) ground-attack version further added to

production delays.

In late 1943, trials began at Peenemünde to see if Heinkel He 111s could be adapted to air-launch V-1 flying-bombs. This led to the He 111H-22 mothership.

1944

Hitler is believed to have sanctioned the possibility of suicide attacks against high-value targets in **March 1944**. From this came the Reichenberg project – air-launched, *manned* V-1 flying-bombs. During the summer of 1944 drop tests we made from He 111s with unpowered Fi 103R-Is, while a batch of nearly 200 warhead-equipped 'R-IVs were manufactured. The plan was dropped in October 1944, co-incidentally just as the Japanese started using conventional fighters in the 'Kamikaze' role against the US Navy. It is unlikely that German high command knew of the intentions of their allies. With conventional landing gear, the Ar 234B V9 had its inaugural flight on **March 10**. Development trials began in June.

The EKdo 262 was established at Rechlin on **April 19** to bring the Me 262A to operational strength as the first frontline turbojet unit. On July 26, the unit claimed its debut 'kill' of a Mosquito.

Eight days after the D-Day landings, on June 13, the first V-1 flying bombs were launched at London from fixed ramp sites in France. The onslaught took on a new dimension on **July 7** when III/KG 53 unleashed V-1s from He 111H-22s that had taken off from bases in the Netherlands. By September the unit had to retreat to German airfields.

A pair of Ar 234 prototypes and two Ar 234B-0s began operations – photo-recce only – first from Rheims in France, then Chièvres in

The Lashenden Air Warfare Museum in Kent has a superbly restored Fieseler Fi 103R-IV Reichenberg on show. It was the aborted suicide version of the flying-bomb. RICHARD FOORD-LAWM WWW.LASHENDENAIRWARFAREMUSEUM.CO.UK

Belgium in July.

Junkers flew the radical four-jet Ju 287 V2 on **August 16.** The month before, the decision had been taken to stop all heavy bomber development, so Junkers was left with a prototype without purpose.

The Ju 287 had a *forward* swept-wing, designed to help both stability and centre of gravity issues, and featured a Jumo 109-004 under each wing and two mounted each side of the forward fuselage. To keep costs down it had a fixed undercarriage and a modified fuselage from a Heinkel He 117. An even more advanced design based on this concept continued almost clandestinely; the unfinished Ju 287 V2 was trucked off to the USSR in May 1945.

Also, on **August 16,** JG 400 attacked a formation of USAAF B-17 Fortresses with its Me 163B-1as – the first operational use of the Komet. The unit had been established at Wittmunhafen in May 1944 to work up on the new type. By May 1945, JG 400 had retreated to Husum, near the Danish border, and was flying infrequently. Despite all that was hoped for the Me 163, by then it had chalked up only nine confirmed 'kills'.

Aimed at Paris, the first in-anger firing of an A4 (V-2) rocket took place on September 5. Four days later London was the target. In total, 1,054 V-2s impacted on Britain, another 1,675 hitting Continental objectives. The last V-2 to hit Britain came down near Orpington in Kent on March 27, 1945.

Major Walter Nowotny's Kommando Nowotny came into being in September, continuing the work of EKdo 262. Also in that month the first Sturmvogel unit, KG 51, which had been established in late June, became operational. On **October 3,** Nowotny's machines engaged USAAF bomber streams for the first time.

Fifteen Bachem Ba 349 Natter (Viper) rocket-powered, vertically launched interceptors were ready for test in October. Manned trials were carried out in glider form, towed by a Heinkel He 111. From late December unmanned vertical launches were initiated. **>**

Below
Ar 234B-2 'FI+MT' of 9/KG 76 was forced down following combat with a USAAF P-47 on February 24, thereby becoming the first of its type the Allies got their hands on. KEY COLLECTION

"Hitler is believed to have sanctioned the possibility of suicide attacks against high-value targets in March 1944. From this came the Reichenberg project – air-launched, *manned* V-1 flying-bombs."

"When the He 162 V1 first flew, there were worries about the plywood elements... Despite this, the programme continued at break-neck pace, the plan being to build 2,000 *per month* by May 1945."

Top
Designed from the outset to use as many non-critical resources as possible, the Heinkel He 162 offered the possibility of being built in huge numbers. PETE WEST © 2014

Above
Dornier's 'push-me, pull you' Do 335 was the ultimate development of the piston-engined fighter. KEC

Given the go-ahead on September 30, 1944, Heinkel rushed the Volksjäger, nicknamed the People's Fighter, into reality. It took to the air on **December 6**. Designed around the BMW 109-003 turbojet and a pair of 20mm cannon, and using as much wood and other non-critical resources as possible, the idea was to create an interceptor that could meet the Allied bombers en masse. To this end, development *and* series production went hand-in-hand.

When the He 162 V1 first flew, there were worries about the plywood elements and four days later (December 10) the V1 crashed fatally due to delamination. Despite this, the programme continued at break-neck pace, the plan being to build 2,000 *per month* by May 1945.

Arado Ar 234Bs hit Liege, Belgium in their operational debut on **December 24**. As recounted in *Wake-up Call* on page 84, Ar 234B-2s of KG 96 bombed Gilze-Rijen in Holland on January 1, 1945. Also in action on New Year's Day was KG 51 with its Me 262A-2s. On February 24, USAAF P-47s engaged an Ar 234, which force landed, allowing the Allies to get their hands on it.

1945
Air-launched V-1 attacks were stopped by KG 53 on **January 14, 1945.** Over 1,200 missiles had been launched, most doing little damage, but 77 He 111 motherships were shot down.

In January, EKdo 162 at Rechlin in Pomerania started operational trials with the He 162. On February 6, JG 1 started to work up on the type and by mid-April 1945 was flying from Leck, near the Danish border (see page 98). The unit was over-run the following month and the He 162's chance to change things had gone; although a staggering 275 had been completed by then.

Lothar Siebert was killed during the first vertical launch of a Ba 349A rocket-powered interceptor in **late February**. There is no record of any further manned trials.

The last V-1 'Doodlebug' dropped on Britain on **March 29**. A total of 9,521 'Doodlebugs' impacted on the country.

As the Third Reich collapsed, British, American and Soviet technicians scoured Luftwaffe airfields and test centres, taking away personnel and equipment for interrogation and trials. The jets and missiles that threatened to tip the balance in World War Two would have to await future conflicts to change the nature of combat. ✚

120231

WINGS OF THE **LUFTWAFFE**

Captain Eric 'Winkle' Brown.

Throughout this publication, the words of the late Captain Eric 'Winkle' Brown CBE DSC AFC RN are quoted, about his experiences of flying Luftwaffe aircraft. The extracts are courtesy of Crécy Publishing which created Eric's book *Wings of the Luftwaffe - Flying the Captured German Aircraft of World War Two* via its Hikoki Publications imprint. Eric died in 2016 aged 97.

During his three decades of flying, Eric flew a staggering 487 different types of aircraft, and in his time at the Royal Aircraft Establishment at Farnborough flew and evaluated Luftwaffe types, ranging from the 'Stuka' to the jets and the Me 163 rocket fighter. In *Wings of the Luftwaffe*, Eric's superb writing style provides a candid; yet technical appraisal of the characteristics of each type in an engaging style. Large format, the 272-page book is lavishly illustrated; with period photos and colour artwork.

Also available from Crécy are two other exceptional works written by Eric, exploring further his exceptional flying career: *Wings of the Navy* and *Wings of the Weird and Wonderful*. All three of these titles are available, at £34.95 each. More details on www.crecy.co.uk

Below
The Messerschmitt Me 262 suffered from changing priorities; was it to be an interceptor, a night-fighter or a fast bomber? This 'B-1a/U1 two-seat trainer was captured by the Americans and given the name 'Vera' before being shipped to the USA.
PETE WEST © 2014

110639

35

Vera

Between them the Royal Air Force Museum's Hendon and Cosford sites contain an impressive collection of former Luftwaffe hardware. Displayed at Hendon is Heinkel He 162A-2 120227 which was delivered to II/JG1 at Leck near the Danish border in April 1945. It may well have been coded 'Red 2' by the time the unit was declared operational at the end of the month, but flying stopped on May 6 as British forces secured the airfield. It was brought to the Royal Aircraft Establishment at Farnborough, Hampshire, but was not flown. It joined the historic aircraft gathered at Colerne, Wiltshire in 1958 and from there became part of the RAF Museum's collection. It was put on show at Hendon in 1989.
KEY-DUNCAN CUBITT